£6·50

TILLING IN LONDON

George Rob

Capital Transport

First published 1986

ISBN 0 904711 82 X

Published by Capital Transport Publishing
38 Long Elmes, Harrow Weald, Middlesex

Printed by Design & Print
Dolphin Road, Shoreham-by-Sea, West Sussex

© Capital Transport Publishing 1986

Photographic Credits

F. Merton Atkins XH 9272.
J.B. Atkinson IT 302.
A.H. Barkway Buses at Old Mill, Plumstead.
Brian Bunker STL 115.
Alan B. Cross STL 70, HPW 95, KHN 498, STL 73, ST 1027, T 311.
Marcus Gaywood LT 743, O 29, O 51, 6111, 6227, STL 64, STL 124 fleetname and legal lettering.
W.J. Haynes XH 9300, STL 555, STL 111, STL 94, STL 58, ST 969.
J.F. Higham O 171, Carswool XR 2120, T 311, 6164, O 145, ST 916, City AGH 149, ST 1010, T315.
W. Noel Jackson XR 3517 (2), XB 9888, XH 9758, XM 2992, XW 9894, XF 9820, O 58, JL YR 1662, Standard
   UW6777, O 44, 963, O 45, 892, UU9161, 6014.
Ben Jenkins XH 9298.
D.W.K. Jones Allitt GN 3185, 6158, STL 104, O 30, ST 882.
C.F. Klapper O 159, STL 554, STL at Bromley South, ST 984.
Lens of Sutton LE 9657 in accident, 36A bus at Grove Park, TTA1s at Red Deer.
London Transport *Frontispiece*, Croydon Garage interior (2), Bromley Garage interior,
   XH 9281 at Piccadilly.
E.G.P. Masterman 47 TTA1 bus at Farnborough, B 5067, O 86, 159C bus at Catford, STL 105, 6225 rear.
Pamlin Prints A 6934 rear, 896 at Old Caterham.
Malcolm Papes Collection 34 bus at Croydon, STL 80, ST 983, STL 113.
Photomatic ST 872.
Purley Library 6115 and XH 9299 at Purley.
Colin Stannard ST 922
Frank Willis ST 950 rear, STL 56, ST 953.
All photos not credited are from the Author's Collection.

Frontispiece Summer 1923, and a busy scene in Regent Street. The Tilling bus in the foreground is number 992, one of the last TS3A buses built and allocated to Croydon garage for routes 59 and 59A. This picture shows the bus in its original condition with very limited protection in front of the driver, but a protective shield was fitted to these buses subsequently. Another Tilling bus on route 12A going to Oxford Circus is trying to overtake. All the other buses seen are K or S type Generals.

Contents

Author's Note

Living in Dulwich in the midst of the Tilling area for so many years enabled me to study the Tilling bus operations in detail. I saw the new buses as they came into service and I soon realised that Tilling kept buses on the same duties each day and I made a careful record of these operations from 1922 onwards, which forms the basis for many of the chapters in this book. There was very little in the way of variation in the TS3A and TS7 Petrol-Electric buses but I recall one on the 78 route, number 890, that had an attractive brass mascot in the shape of a bird with outstretched wings on the radiator cap. Another bus, number 918 on the 12A service, had disc wheels instead of the normal spoked wheels of those days. I was fortunate in meeting the late Harry Webb who had been employed by Tilling for most of his working life, first as a horse bus conductor, later as an inspector and eventually as Traffic Manager in motor days. He supplied me with much valuable information on Tilling's early days and his diary of events in the history of Tilling routes and operations has been a great help to me.

The story shows that apart from routes like 47 and 75, which had been started by Tilling prior to 1913, operations by the Company's buses were on routes that had originated with the LGOC. I would draw attention to Tilling's system of operation, whereby bus crews kept to the same bus all the time, a system inherited from horse bus days. Joint working with the LGOC meant that the system had to be modified and that the men had to work on more than one bus. But the company continued with the practice of keeping buses to the same duties each day, replaced by a spare when necessary. This continued until the LPTB took over Tilling's operations. Throughout the years of joint working, Tilling managed to operate a maximum number of buses, seven days a week, summer and winter, taking over additional duties from General to complete the schedules.

I wish to acknowledge the help given to me by members of the London Historical Research Group of the Omnibus Society, not forgetting the late Albert McCall and the late Charles E. Lee, who had followed closely the development of Tilling's motor services and was known personally to most of the directors of the Company and to many of the officials. The story has been continued after Tilling days, and I am grateful for the help given by Brian Bunker, Les Stitson and Malcolm Papes with the later chapters. Finally I wish to thank Reg Durrant, the Ticket Curator of the Omnibus Society for kindly supplying information and photographs of the tickets used by Thomas Tilling on motor buses.

Taunton, August 1986   GEORGE J. ROBBINS

1 Early Motor Bus Operation 1904-1911

This photo of a Tilling horse bus on the Clapham Junction and Raynes Park route was taken on 1st May 1903 and the conductor standing behind the vehicle is the late Harry Webb, whose diary of events forms the basis for much of the early part of this story. The curtains at the windows were not normal even in horse bus days.

The large Tilling organisation stemmed from a jobmasters business which was started in London in 1847 by Thomas Tilling. He was born on 3rd February 1825 at Gutter Edge Farm in Hendon and he began business in 1845 when he bought a dairying concern in Walworth. His transport business started on 12th May 1847 when he obtained a horse and carriage for hiring purposes. The first bus wholly owned and worked by Tilling was purchased in December 1849 from Mr William Stevens. This was a four-horsed vehicle named the 'Times' and it ran from Peckham (Rye Lane) to the 'Green Man and Still' on the north side of Oxford Street. It worked four journeys daily, Thomas himself driving the first one each morning. From this small beginning, Tilling's horse buses made most spectacular progress during the subsequent 50 years, and at the height of the horse bus era Tilling owned 7,000 horses and 250 horse buses. In addition to the hauling of the buses, horses were supplied for cabs and other vehicles and for riding. Several new routes were commenced as late as 1898 and 1899, and on 1st January 1901 Tilling had 220 horse buses in regular use.

Three years later, although further development had taken place in Tilling's horse bus routes and a record number of horses were owned, it was realised that horse power must inevitably give way to the motor. At that time motor buses were still at an experimental stage and few had been successful or had lasted long in service.

A Tilling horse bus working on the Lewisham and City route that served Rotherhithe and Bermondsey. It was replaced in July 1912 by new motor bus route numbered 47 and running between Bromley Market Place and Shoreditch.

The Dulwich and Liverpool Street horse buses bore the fleetname PECKHAM as seen by this bus on the 'Plough' stand at Dulwich. This service was the forerunner of motor bus route 78, Shoreditch and Dulwich, which commenced in 1913. The boards on the side read 'OVER TOWER BRIDGE' and 'DULWICH PARK' though the park is some distance from this point. Most horse buses carried adverts for Nestles Milk and Hudsons Soap.

This rear view of Milnes-Daimler A 6934, Tillings first motor bus, shows the vehicle in brilliant condition as it stands outside the Peckham Works. The use of curtains at the windows was not continued.

The Tilling company chose one of the then most reliable of the chassis to promote their motor bus operation. Thomas Tilling himself had not lived to see this change as he died in 1893 and the business was being carried on by his sons Richard and Edward Tilling and their brother-in-law Walter Wolsey. They continued in partnership until the business was converted into a limited company on 12th May 1897. It was mainly Richard Tilling who was responsible for the progress made in the early motor days.

The chosen chassis was a 24hp Milnes-Daimler which was fitted with a Birch-built 34-seat body, having 16 longitudinal seats inside and 18 garden seats outside on the top deck. This was to be the motor bus standard for many years. Solid rubber tyres, acetylene lighting and curtains to the windows were important features, though the curtains did not appear subsequently. It was the first orthodox double-deck bus to be built for public service in London. In order to introduce it, the directors of Thomas Tilling Ltd (the proprietors) and Milnes-Daimler Ltd (the constructors) issued an invitation requesting the pleasure of the company of numerous distinguished persons at the inaugural trip of the motor bus on Wednesday 28th September 1904. The arrangements for the inaugural trip provided for the motor bus leaving Winchester House, Peckham (the Company's headquarters) at 12.30pm for a run to Oxford Circus which was to be reached by about 1.05pm. Long

before midday, a considerable crowd had assembled in front of the 'Kentish Drovers' in Peckham High Street to cheer the bus on its way. According to the South London Press of the following Saturday, the inaugural trip was actually made in 20 minutes. After lunch, the return to Peckham was made via the City, London Bridge and the Borough. In Throgmorton Street, the bus was cheered by members of the Stock Exchange.

The Police licence (plate number 3157) was granted on 29th September and the bus went into service the next day, Friday 30th September, on the 'Times' route between the 'Dolphin' in Oxford Street and Peckham High Street, where the bus turned round at the end of Rye Lane. The route ran via Westminster, Elephant & Castle and Camberwell Green. Although working on the 'Times' route, the new motor bus no longer carried that name on the side as had been the practice with the horse buses. Instead, the legend 'PECKHAM & OXFORD ST' was shown on the sides on an emerald green board. The livery adopted for the motor bus bodies was all one colour, namely dark green with gold mouldings. The rockers and wheels were yellow, the staircase black, the bonnet dark green and the canopy red. The fare from Peckham to Piccadilly was 2½d and to Oxford Street 3d. This first bus, which carried the registration number A 6934, was so successful that the Company placed an order for another 24 Milnes Daimlers, and numbers 2 and 3 were delivered before the end of the year.

A 6934 seen on 28th September 1904 on its inaugural run over the 'TIMES' route between Peckham and Oxford Street. The roller blind for the ultimate destination is carried high enough to clear advertisements when they are shown on the bus.

Tillings were members of the Atlas and Waterloo Omnibus Association, which was formed many years earlier to protect the interests of member horse bus operators by combating competition and allocating a definite place for each bus on its route. These places were known as 'times' and they could be bought and sold.

In September 1904, when the first motor bus entered regular service, there were 30 horse buses on the 'Times' route. Other operators shared the route with Tilling, all members of the Atlas and Waterloo Omnibus Association. Tilling supplied 22 buses, and the rest came from C. French, Pat Hearn, Tom Hearne, F. Newman, H. Turner, and the Star Omnibus Company. Most of these horse bus proprietors followed the lead given by Tillings and introduced motor buses; P. Hearn and T. Hearne used Milnes-Daimlers, F. Newman De Dions, whilst the Star bought a Brillé. The replacement of horse buses by motor buses on Association routes was governed by an agreement whereby two horse buses would be withdrawn in exchange for one motor bus.

Tilling continued to replace horse buses on the 'Times' route during 1905 and the new Milnes-Daimlers were placed in service as follows:

31st December 1904
4 'Times' buses taken off, leaving 18
2 motors introduced the following day
12th February 1905
4 'Times' buses taken off, leaving 14
2 motors introduced; total 4
19th March 1905
4 'Times' buses taken off, leaving 10
2 motors introduced; total 6
21st April 1905
4 'Times' buses taken off, leaving 6
2 motors introduced; total 8
23rd July 1905
2 'Times' buses taken off, leaving 4
1 motor introduced; total 9
20th August 1905
2 'Times' buses taken off, leaving 2
1 motor introduced, total 10
16th December 1905
2 'Times' buses taken off, leaving none
2 motors introduced, total 12.

Milnes-Daimler A 8649, Tilling's No. 4, is here standing in Peckham High Street before setting off for Oxford Street. The Nestles' Milk advertisements so familiar on the horse buses have found a place on the motor buses.

This Dennis bus, LC 3128, was on trial in December 1905 and is seen outside the Talbot Hotel just four days before Christmas. It was operated on the Lee Green and Peckham service, but both bus and route were withdrawn by April 1906.

During 1905 the motor fleet was increased to 20 Milnes-Daimlers by the gradual delivery of the order placed the previous year. Three chassis were used for vans for the Royal Mail service between London and Brighton and the first of these ran on 2nd June 1905. There was a breakdown lorry on a secondhand chassis and 16 of the remainder were in use as buses. They were numbered 1 to 20, only one series being used for buses and other motor vehicles. All 20 were kept at the Bull Yard, Peckham which had been adapted as a motor bus garage. These premises had first been leased by Thomas Tilling in 1876, when only the west part of the yard was acquired. Richard Tilling leased the centre and south in 1896, and the east part the next year. In the early years petrol storage was simply in two gallon cans, but on 31st March 1905 Tilling was granted a licence to construct four tanks with a total capacity of 1,000 gallons for Bull Yard. This is believed to be the first example of bulk petrol storage for a bus company.

Tilling were fortunate in February 1905 when they were able to gain the services of Percy Frost Smith as Engineer. He was highly skilled and contributed to the early success of the service. By the end of the year, thirteen buses were working on the 'Times' route leaving three to cover for breakdowns and overhauls, and thus it was possible to maintain a regular service. Tilling did, of course, experiment with makes of bus other than Milnes-Daimler as well. In May 1905 a Büssing was on trial, and this was followed in January 1906 by a Dennis which worked on a new service between Peckham and Lee Green. By April, both the bus and the route had been withdrawn. These two buses were not given a number in the Tilling fleet.

The other operators gradually left the 'Times' service; first C. French withdrew his buses for another route so that Tillings were able to place further motors on to the route, one on 11th March 1906 and another on 25th of same month, bringing their total to 15. The other five operators transferred their buses to another route on 1st July 1906, although four of them set up a new route in competition between Marylebone Station and Peckham. Three of them ceased during 1907, but F. Newman continued with De Dions until 6th February 1909. After Tilling had become the sole operator on the 'Times' route, it terminated its sharing agreement with the Atlas and Waterloo Association on 15th December 1906. More direct competition appeared on 11th February 1907 when a new contender, the Amalgamated Omnibus Company entered the fray by placing a Brush motor bus on the Oxford Circus to Peckham route. A second Brush followed in March, a third in April, a fourth in June, and finally a fifth in the August of the next year. All were withdrawn from the route late in 1908.

Tilling began another route on Sunday 14th January 1906 when one Milnes-Daimler was placed on a Lewisham to Peckham service. It was probably the first regular motor bus route to be worked exclusively in the suburbs without approaching any central London point. A second motor was put on this route on 18th February.

Between February and April 1906 another five Milnes-Daimlers were licensed for service, thus completing the 24 ordered in 1904, and then during May and June 1906 six Straker-Squire buses were added to the fleet. Two more buses were put on to the Lewisham to Peckham route on 6th May and three more three weeks later, bringing the total to seven. On 10th June

Top **Another route served by the Milnes-Daimlers was that between Catford and Greenwich Pier, which started on 17th June 1906. This picture of No. 28 shows that the side advertisement had been changed in order to draw attention to Tilling's being motor carriage proprietors.** Above **During May and June 1906, six Straker-Squire/Büssings had been added to the fleet and operated on the Lewisham and Peckham route as this picture shows.**

the LCC Greenwich and Catford horse tram service was cut back at Lewisham Obelisk and new electric trams covered the remainder of the route to Catford. One week later on Sunday 17th June, Tilling placed a Milnes-Daimler on another new route, between Catford and Greenwich Pier; thus providing a through connection between the two points. Tillings tended to start new routes or to put new buses into service on Sundays. One more bus was added to the Greenwich route a week later and two more from Sunday 15th July. On Thursday 28th June the Peckham and Lewisham route was extended to Catford (Rushey Green) providing further competition with the electric trams. In July a new garage was opened at Lewisham for which the buses operating on this route, six and one spare, were transferred. The Strakers were in use on this service. Lewisham garage, known as Salisbury Yard, was acquired by Tilling in 1899 and used for building horse buses. It was situated between High Street and Molesworth Street. It was in use as a bus garage from 1906 until October 1920, when it reverted to building work.

On 26th September 1906, two of the motor buses operating the 'Times' service started running extra late journeys leaving Oxford Street after 1.00am to cater for the service staff at hotels and restaurants. By the end of this eventful year, the Tilling motor bus fleet stood at 32 vehicles; 26 Milnes-Daimlers and six Straker-

Early in 1907 six Dennis buses were obtained and the first of these was No. 55, LC 3617, seen here in February 1907 on a test run before entering service. It carries an advertisement for TATCHO hair restorer, shown on all Tilling buses at that time but a product unknown today.

Squires. On order were six Tylor engined Dennis buses. Three routes were operated: 15 buses on the 'Times' route, running between Peckham and Oxford Street, four buses on the Catford to Greewich Pier service, and four buses only on the Peckham to Catford service. The last two routes were worked from the Lewisham garage.

In the first four months of 1907, another nine buses were added to the fleet. Five of these were Milnes-Daimlers and the rest were the first four of the Dennis order mentioned previously. It was thus possible from 17th March to add two more buses to the Catford and Greenwich Pier service bringing the total to six, and then three weeks later the sixteenth bus was added to the 'Times' service.

Such rapid growth was bound to need some readjustment, and this came about on Sunday 28th July 1907. The Catford to Greenwich and Peckham to Catford services were discontinued, and four buses were removed from the 'Times' service, leaving 12 in all on that road. A new route was commenced using 13 buses between Oxford Street and Sidcup (Black Horse). This ran jointly with the 'Times' route from Oxford Street to Peckham and then continued via Lewisham and Lee Green. It was 15 miles long, and it is likely that Tilling could lay claim to the longest route in London at that time. A 15-minute headway was maintained. The complexity of the fare structure meant that every ticket from ½d to 9d could be issued and, in all, 159 different fares were involved. Obviously there was some difficulty in providing a clear fare table of the format in normal use by General and Tilling, which was laid out in a 'block system' whereby each fare point was listed in order followed by all the fares from that point. Thus, a new form of chart faretable was introduced to overcome this mass of fare possibilities, and it is interesting that it became the standard for the LGOC some 20 years later, this company adopting it in January 1927. This formed the basis of the typical chart still in use today.

During June 1907, the remaining two Dennis buses were licensed, bringing the total motor buses for Tilling to 43, although at any one time seldom more than 35 were licensed. The majority were Milnes-Daimlers, of which 31 had been put on the road and several more obtained for use as Royal Mail vans. The six Straker-Squire buses new in 1906 were withdrawn from service in May 1907 for some modifications and did not return to service until 1908. The six Dennis buses new in 1907 were also withdrawn after a few months in service and modified between November and July of 1908. Some Milnes-Daimlers were converted to chain drive during 1907 and 1908, and also fitted with HT magnetos. Most of the early ones were later converted to vans and transferred to the Royal Mail fleet being used between London and Dover, Birmingham, Southampton or Ipswich.

In January 1908 Tilling introduced a new type of bus to London, a petrol-electric omnibus built after much experimental work at the Bull Yard works in an attempt to produce a more reliable vehicle. It was called 'Queenie' by the men because it behaved so well, but officially it was known as the SB&S type after the joint inventors, Percy Frost Smith, Engineer and Manager of Tilling's Motor Department, Frank Brown (Chairman of David Brown and Sons Ltd of Huddersfield), makers of the final drive, and W.A. Stevens (Managing Director of W.A. Stevens Ltd of Maidstone), who designed the electric transmission. The bus had a petrol engine driving a dynamo, the current being fed to two motors slung outside the main frame. Each motor drove one of the rear wheels by means of a carden shaft.

This first petrol-electric was slow in starting and it was difficult to work up to the permitted speed of 12mph. Nevertheless, there was a summons against a driver for travelling at 16mph in St George's Road, and despite expert evidence that it was practically impossible for this speed to be attained, there was a conviction. This experimental SB&S bus was numbered 73 in the Tilling fleet and operated the 'Times' route weekdays and the Sidcup service on Sundays. The experience gained with this bus over 60,000 miles of work on London streets caused various adjustments to be made with the result that an improved petrol-electric vehicle was marketed under the name of Halford-Stevens, but none were operated by Tilling.

For nearly two years from July 1907, Tilling's motor buses ran with little change on the two main services, 12 buses (reduced to ten from October 1907) on the Oxford Street to Peckham route and 13 buses on Oxford Street to Sidcup.

An important development took place in London on 1st July 1908 which was to have considerable effect on Tilling's future. This was the amalgamation of the London Road Car Company and the London Motor Omnibus Company (Vanguard) with the London General Omnibus Company, thus giving the latter a fleet of over 900 buses working on 20 well-established routes. The LGOC thereby became a much larger and formidable competitor. Ten months later, on 6th May 1909, came the first joint working with the LGOC following a sharing agreement entered into between the two companies, and thereafter Tilling's motors were worked under this agreement. Ten Tilling buses on the Peckham to Oxford Street service with one extra bus added were extended northwards to Harringay (Queens Head) and a similar number of General buses, namely P type Büssings from Old Kent Road garage, ran on the route, which was allocated the number 13 in the LGOC series. This was the first time that Tilling buses had carried a service number and it was shown in the same way as on the Generals, a black number on a white circular board fixed below the route board on the driver's

canopy. For reasons unknown, this joint working did not last long, as on 16th September 1909 the General buses were withdrawn and the 11 Tillings resumed the Oxford Street to Peckham operation.

There followed a period of six months with no change as far as Tilling was concerned, and then on 20th March 1910 the Oxford Circus to Peckham service was extended to Bromley (Market Place) via New Cross, Lewisham and Catford. A fare chart similar to that prepared for the Sidcup route had been produced for this extension back in 1907. The number 13 was used again for this service, and at the same time the Oxford Circus to Sidcup route was allotted the number 21. The venture lasted only a few months, and on 12th December 1910 both the Bromley and Sidcup routes were discontinued and their vehicles redistributed as follows: 15 Milnes-Daimler and the SB&S from Bull Yard on the Oxford Street to Peckham route, six Straker-Squires or Milnes-Daimlers on the Lewisham to Sidcup route and four Dennis on the Lewisham to Bromley route, both from Lewisham garage. The last two routes operated from Oxford Circus on Sundays. The use of the route numbers 13 and 21 was discontinued and the LGOC reused number 13 for a different route of its own immediately and used the number 21 again a few months later. A relief service of two buses was added to the Lewisham to Sidcup route from 9th January 1911.

'Queenie' was the name given by the crews to this SB&S bus, so smooth was its operation. Numbered 78 and registered as LC 3627 it was the first petrol-electric bus produced in January 1908 and it ran successfully on the Peckham and Oxford Street route.

During 1910 Tilling buses worked between Oxford Street and Bromley (Market Place) using the service number 13, and two Dennis buses are seen on the route. The board reading 'CAMBERWELL/ ELEPHANT/ WESTMINSTER BRIDGE' was also used for the TIMES route, of which this was an extension.

The other long-distance route operated by Tilling in 1910 was the 21 between Sidcup and Oxford Street. The same limited route board is seen on this bus, a Milnes-Daimler standing outside the 'Black Horse' at Sidcup. By this time Tilling buses were carrying a running number, in this case 11.

The late Mr H. Webb, who spent a lifetime working for Tilling including these early years of motor bus operation, supplied some illuminating recollections regarding the Oxford Circus to Peckham route. He said that there was no standing for the early motor buses at Oxford Street; it was a turning point only. The system was that buses set down passengers in Regent Street just beyond Maddox Street. The timekeeper then instructed the drivers to turn left into Oxford Street and take the first or second turning on the right as the case may be, to secure adequate spacing on departure. At Peckham, public toilets were situated in the middle of the High Street just before its junction with Rye Lane, and two buses stood crossways in the road at the far end of these conveniences. The timekeeper stood in the centre and dispatched the buses according to circumstances rather than time schedule.

If the early motor buses were unduly noisy, belched too much smoke, or were otherwise considered to be defective, a 'stop' notice would be served by the police on the proprietor who had to take the bus out of service and not operate it again until it was passed fit by a Police Public Carriage Officer. Occasionally, officials from Scotland Yard in plain clothes stood on one of the road islands in Whitehall, and made a note of any offending vehicle. Tilling called them the 'Noise Committee' and, when they were about, diverted their buses via Embankment and Northumberland Avenue, thus avoiding scrutiny. Regarding the 'opposition', the two De Dion buses operated by F. Newman were the most reliable. Their drivers had the almost uncanny knack of being able to right any failings quickly, and regular passengers got to know this so that a full load was assured from the starting point. On these occasions they ran through Southampton Street and Addington Square to avoid Camberwell Green, which was a busy point even in those days. This excellent reputation could hardly be claimed for the buses of another 'opposition' member, the Star Company who had introduced a fleet of French Brillé buses. They were compact looking buses but did not stand up well in service, and if they attained any speed at all, parts were apt to fall off in the road. They must indeed have been an unprofitable investment for the Star.

Mr Webb went on to consider the 'Times' service. It was worked from the Bull Yard, which had originally got its name from the 'Bull' public house situated in Peckham High Street. There was an opening between this pub and the neighbouring shops which allowed access to the Yard so that a motor bus could easily pass through. It was originally used as stables with housing for horse buses and it was converted to hold 35 motor buses together with some workshops. Later some property and ground in Hanover Park were purchased and the garage was extended.

The 'Times' service worked for nearly 20 hours daily, the first bus leaving Peckham at 6.30am, and the last arriving about 2.00am next day. This last bus which was scheduled to leave Oxford Street at 1.15am was often later by request when important events were on at the local hotels. It was usually well-laden with waiters and other hotel workers. The crew were given a good tip for delaying departure on special occasions.

Each bus was scheduled to work 12 journeys covered by early and late shifts doing six journeys each. Wages were six shillings (30p) per day if three or more journeys were worked. The minimum fare from Oxford Circus to Piccadilly Circus was one old penny, but from Charing Cross southward the faretable was split into halfpenny sections, many of which covered a mile. In 1909 the threehalfpenny fare from Peckham to St Thomas's Hospital was extended to Whitehall (Parliament Street), a distance of a good three miles.

Tilling adopted their own method of route identification commencing with their very first motor bus. The extreme destination was shown on a roller blind fitted in a box mounted on two iron poles fixed to the canopy over the driver's cab. This was in the front only and read either 'PECKHAM' or 'OXFORD ST'. Route identification was by means of coloured boards slotted in on either side below the lower deck windows. These boards gave the two terminals and two or three names denoting the route. With horse buses, the whole vehicle had been painted in different colours to identify the route, but with motor buses these boards sufficed. The motor bus bodies were all in one livery, dark green with gold mouldings. Rockers and wheels were yellow picked out in black, the staircase and bonnet were dark green and the canopy was red.

The colours of these side boards were as follows:

PECKHAM & OXFORD ST
Emerald green with large letters blocked red and white and small letters black with double shadow.
LEE GREEN & PECKHAM
Emerald green, edged dark green, with fine line of white. Square gold letters blocked red and white.
LEWISHAM & PECKHAM
Vermilion, edged in dark green, with fine line of white. Square gold letters blocked blue and white.
CATFORD & GREENWICH PIER
Same as for Lee Green & Peckham.

SIDCUP & OXFORD ST
Vermilion with square gold, black-shadowed letters.
PECKHAM & CATFORD
Same as for Lewisham & Peckham.
BROMLEY & OXFORD ST
Dark green and grey.
HARRINGAY & PECKHAM
Dark green and orange.
SIDCUP & LEWISHAM
Same as Sidcup & Oxford St.
BROMLEY & LEWISHAM
Same as Bromley & Oxford St.

Front boards fitted to the driver's canopy and showing three places en route were fitted later.

The faretables for these were laid out thus:

RYE LANE, PECKHAM.									
½	TOWN HALL, CAMBERWELL								
1	½	CAMBERWELL GREEN							
1	1	½	NEW CHURCH ROAD						
1	1	½	½	CAMBERWELL GATE					
1½	1	1	½	½	MANOR PLACE				
1½	1	1	1	½	½	ELEPHANT			
1½	1½	1	1	1	1	½	ST THOMAS HOSPITAL		
2	2	1½	1½	1	1	1	½	CHARING CROSS	
2½	2½	2	2	2	2	1½	1	1	PICCADILLY CIRCUS
3	3	2½	2½	2	2	2	1½	1	1	OXFORD STREET

EXAMPLE OF CHART FORM OF
FARETABLE FOR 'TIMES' ROUTE

ALTERNATIVE BLOCK SYSTEM

RYE LANE, PECKHAM and
TOWN HALL, CAMBERWELL	½
CAMBERWELL GREEN	1
NEW CHURCH ROAD	1
CAMBERWELL GATE	1
MANOR PLACE	1½
ELEPHANT	1½
ST THOMAS HOSPITAL	1½
CHARING CROSS	2
PICCADILLY CIRCUS	2½
OXFORD STREET	3

TOWN HALL, CAMBERWELL and
CAMBERWELL GREEN	½
NEW CHURCH ROAD	1
CAMBERWELL GATE	1
MANOR PLACE	1
ELEPHANT	1
ST THOMAS HOSPITAL	1½
CHARING CROSS	2
PICCADILLY CIRCUS	2½
OXFORD STREET	3

CAMBERWELL GREEN and
NEW CHURCH ROAD	½
CAMBERWELL GATE	½
MANOR PLACE	1
ELEPHANT	1
ST THOMAS HOSPITAL	1
CHARING CROSS	1½
PICCADILLY CIRCUS	2
OXFORD STREET	2½

NEW CHURCH ROAD and
CAMBERWELL GATE	½
MANOR PLACE	½
ELEPHANT	1
ST THOMAS HOSPITAL	1
CHARING CROSS	1½
PICCADILLY CIRCUS	2
OXFORD STREET	2½

CAMBERWELL GATE and
MANOR PLACE	½
ELEPHANT	½
ST THOMAS HOSPITAL	1
CHARING CROSS	1
PICCADILLY CIRCUS	2
OXFORD STREET	2

MANOR PLACE and
ELEPHANT	½
ST THOMAS HOSPITAL	1
CHARING CROSS	1
PICCADILLY CIRCUS	2
OXFORD STREET	2

ELEPHANT and
ST THOMAS HOSPITAL	½
CHARING CROSS	1
PICCADILLY CIRCUS	1½
OXFORD STREET	2

ST THOMAS HOSPITAL and
CHARING CROSS	½
PICCADILLY CIRCUS	1
OXFORD STREET	1½

CHARING CROSS and
PICCADILLY CIRCUS	1
OXFORD STREET	1

PICCADILLY CIRCUS and
OXFORD STREET	1

2 Tilling and the London Bus Combine 1911-1914

Sharing and joint operation with the LGOC was resumed in earnest in May 1911 due to the severe competition both companies were experiencing from the National Steam Car Company Ltd, which had begun in 1909 with a route from Shepherds Bush to Westminster Bridge Road. Gradually they had built up a fleet of Clarkson steam buses painted white and in May 1910 the route was extended over the 'Times' route to Peckham High Street (Rye Lane). By that time they had about nine buses on the road but by 20th February 1911 the fleet had increased to 20 and the route was extended down Rye Lane to terminate at Peckham Rye (King's Arms). National also opened a new bus garage in Nunhead Lane near that point.

In order to combat this competition, LGOC diverted its number 12 route (Turnham Green and Liverpool Street) at Oxford Circus and extended it to Peckham High Street on Monday 8th May 1911. Tilling's Peckham and Oxford Street route was also extended to Turnham Green, operating as service 12. It thus became a joint working, and whilst LGOC used 24 of their new B type buses from the newly-opened garage at Turnham Green (V), Tilling operated 16 buses, 15 Milnes-Daimlers and the SB&S. One extra bus had been added to the 15 which had been taken from the 'Times' route. The Tilling vehicles were painted dark green and carried the legend 'PECKHAM & TURNHAM GREEN' on the sides. This joint working applied only on weekdays, as General continued their own Sunday operation of route 12 between Richmond and Shoreditch, whilst Tilling covered the remainder of the route with their own special Sunday services, Oxford Circus to Sidcup and Oxford Circus to Bromley.

This joint working was connected with decisions made earlier that month. The LGOC board meeting on 4th May 1911 was attended by Richard S. Tilling and Walter Wolsey Jr, who explained that Frost Smith and two others had a patent petrol-electric transmission that Thomas Tilling had an option to buy for £3,000; that the Daimler company's KPL bus infringed this, and that Daimler had offered to purchase the rights from the patentees for £5,000. Daimler's first bus had been produced in 1906, using the petrol-electric system of Henri Pieper of Liege. In 1910 the KPL, another petrol-electric, was produced under the patents of Knight, Pieper and Lanchester. Although worked experimentally, neither went into production, but Richard Tilling suggested that it might be in the interests of the LGOC to purchase the patent owing to the fact that the patentees wanted it to be used by a new company to operate petrol-electric buses in London. The matter was referred to the LGOC's solicitors for advice and considered at the next board meeting on 11th May, when the directors at the request of Richard Tilling

The experience gained with the SB&S bus resulted in the development of the famous TTA1 petrol-electric vehicle which served Tilling so well for over a decade. The first bus, LN 9998, painted green with yellow panels and sloping bonnet, entered service on the Peckham and Turnham Green route in June 1911. In the petrol-electric system, a petrol dynamo powered an electric motor which drove the rear wheels. It was simpler to operate because no gears were necessary. One lever was used to select forward, reverse or neutral and another controlled the vehicle's speed.

resolved that the LGOC should provide the £3,000 for the purchase of the rights under the patent in an attempt to prevent any new company being established. In view of Tilling's own plans to expand their fleet by placing in service a substantial number of petrol-electrics, the LGOC received in return from Tilling an undertaking that their weekday scheduled total of motor buses would not at any time exceed 150, a figure which would represent about 5% of total bus operation in London and which was over four times the size of Tilling's fleet in May 1911. A form of joint working was also agreed for cases where the LGOC wished to extend any of its routes into the Tilling area. A comprehensive agreement between the two companies followed a year later.

Although an objection to the patent by the Daimler company was found to be valid, the flotation of the proposed company was postponed and eventually abandoned. Tilling, committed to the petrol-electric system, designed a new type of bus based on the experience gained with the SB&S which was to become their main class of vehicle for the next ten years. This was the TTA1 petrol-electric which was built in the workshops of the Bull Yard with electrical equipment by W.A. Stevens of Maidstone. It was unusual in having a sloping Renault-type bonnet. It had a 30hp engine with a bore of 125mm, the dynamo being coupled to the engine by the means of a pair of laminated springs lying transversely across the flywheel. The 34-seat body was built at the Company's bodyworks at Wren Road, Camberwell. The first TTA1 was painted green, the chassis and lower panel were yellow, but the livery was soon changed to an overall red with brown chassis. The fleetname 'Thos TILLING Ltd' was carried, and route boards similar to those standard to the General with six lines of detail were fitted front and back. Another board of the route detail covered the top of the windows and the words 'PECKHAM & TURNHAM GREEN' were shown along the top deck sides. The service number, still in the round white style, was fitted to the centre of the driver's canopy at the front and at the back on top of the rear nearside window post.

A demonstration run of the new TTA1 was made on Friday 2nd June 1911 and the vehicle went into public service on 11th June. As this was a Sunday, its first revenue earning journeys were made on the Oxford Circus to Sidcup route. It started to work route 12 the next day, becoming the seventeenth Tilling bus on that service.

Competition with National Steam Car Company was fierce. LGOC put an extra six B type buses onto route 12 on 2nd October 1911 and then, three days later, the route was extended from Peckham High Street down Rye Lane to Peckham Rye (King's Arms), a point to which National had attained some months earlier. Tilling also felt it worthwhile to contribute another three buses, bringing their total to 20 by taking off three extras that had worked on the Sidcup and Bromley routes. The LGOC, having more of their new B type available, decided to flood the route; by 16th October they had increased their allocation from 30 to 46, thus making a total of 66 vehicles altogether in competition with 30 National steam buses.

In late-October 1911 a new garage was opened by Tilling at Arch Street just north of New Kent Road near to the Elephant and Castle, and the allocation of 20 buses for route 12 was transferred to it from Bull Yard, which then became the headquarters for manufacture and vehicle repair. The combined General and Tilling allocation of buses enabled the 12 route to run every three minutes on weekdays, and commencing 15th October 1911 the LGOC provided a 12-minute service on Sundays between Turnham Green and Peckham Rye. The Richmond to Shoreditch Sunday operation was continued separately under the number 57. Tilling was so pleased with the new vehicles that after only six had entered service in November 1911 they proposed to withdraw all their gear-driven buses and replace them with petrol-electrics. One reason was that the absence of a clutch made it easier for former horse bus drivers to be trained to drive motor buses. Although at first the TTA1s were built at Bull Yard, production was soon transferred to Maidstone in Kent under the aegis of a new company, Tilling-Stevens Ltd, which was formed when Tilling gained financial control of W.A. Stevens Ltd in 1912. The new type of bus soon became very popular and buses were being built for other operators, the first in May 1912 for Birmingham & Midland Motor Omnibus Company, later popularly known as 'Midland Red'.

Above A new garage (Arch Street) for the TTA1 buses working on the 12 route was opened in October 1911 and two buses are seen outside the garage one Sunday morning. Although carrying route number 12 they are preparing to set out for the special Sunday operation to Sidcup.

Waiting to pick up passengers at Turnham Green is TTA1 LE 9556, although the route board has not been turned correctly in the direction of travel for the journey to Peckham. The running number (17) has been moved to a new position beside the driver's seat.

15

By May 1912, thirty-five new TTA1 buses had been built and licensed by the company and these replaced all the older buses on route 12 as well as ten buses at Lewisham garage on the Bromley and Sidcup services. Early in May 1912, another new garage was opened by Tilling at Victory Place just south of New Kent Road, and the 25 buses used on the 12 service and the Sunday Sidcup route were transferred to it, leaving the Arch Street premises to be used exclusively for the growing commercial fleet under contract to Tilling. Following the introduction of motor buses, Tilling commenced to promote the use of motor vehicles for commercial transport and in 1906 operated a number of Panhard taxicabs. They obtained many contracts for housing and maintaining motor vans for various companies. Numerous types of chassis were bought and the vans were of differing sizes according to their use. Many of their bodies were built by Tilling at their coachbuilding works, first at Salisbury Yard, Lewisham and then, when that became a bus garage, at Wren Road, Camberwell. It is known they built a small box-like body on a landaulette chassis which was hired by Peck, the potted meat firm near the Old Kent Road. Tilling was successful in securing a large number of contracts and many well-known business concerns used vans which were painted in their own individual colours though looked after by Tilling — W.H. Smith; Cadburys; McFarlane Lang Biscuits; Barclay Perkins (Brewers); James Keiller; Waterman's Fountain Pens; and many others. These motor vehicles were all numbered in the same sequence as the motor buses and this accounts for the many gaps in the numbering of the fleet.

The new agreement between Tilling and LGOC dated 15th May 1912 led to further London bus routes being worked jointly by the two companies. The first of these commenced on 23rd May 1912 when Tilling's Sidcup to Lewisham route was extended to Victoria via Peckham and Camberwell Green and acquired route number 39. In addition to the six buses working from Lewisham garage, six more were taken off route 12 from Victory Place garage, and these joined route 39 at Camberwell Green, thus providing a bus every 16 minutes. One month later on 20th June 1912, General provided 12 B type buses from Old Kent Road garage (P) thus making a total of 24 buses and increasing the frequency to every seven or eight minutes. With the loss of the six buses to the 39, the headway on the 12 route was widened to every 4-5 minutes as the LGOC reduced its number of buses to 32 and Tilling to 14.

The next change resulted in the extension of a General route into the Tilling territory. This took place on 20th June 1912 when the 36 (West Kilburn and Victoria) was extended to Catford via Camberwell Green and New Cross. Tilling placed six new TTA1 buses from Lewisham garage on the service, whilst LGOC provided 26 B type from its Kilburn garage (K). The route had originally been started in July 1909 by the Great Eastern London Motor Omnibus Company Ltd. This Company was taken over by LGOC on 6th April 1911 and the route was then numbered 36 and extended to Elephant & Castle. On 13th September 1911, it was extended to Liverpool Street but later cut back to Victoria. The General alone operated the 36 and 39 routes on Sundays as Tilling continued the Sunday working on the Oxford Circus to Bromley route. Similarly, 16 buses from Victory Place off the 12 route ran on Sundays between Oxford Circus and Sidcup. These two Sunday routes were at that time

allocated numbers in the LGOC Sunday series as 63 (the Sidcup route) and 64 (Bromley).

During the next 12 months another 100 TTA1 type buses were built and licensed for Thomas Tilling and as they became available four new bus routes were introduced. These routes were initially entirely Tilling operated and not joint with General, and the first three covered certain parts of the Tilling horse bus routes. The first of these new routes started on Saturday 20th July 1912 when the Bromley to Lewisham motor bus route was extended north to Shoreditch via Deptford and London Bridge to replace the Lewisham and City horse bus route, 17 horse buses having been withdrawn on the previous day. The new route was numbered 47, and 13 TTA1s were used, nine from Lewisham garage (an additional four having been added to the Bromley service on July 4th) and four from Victory Place. The latter came off route 39 which was then entirely worked by Lewisham. By this time the 12 route had been increased to 16 buses. Two more Lewisham buses were put on the 47 by 1st August.

During 1912, LGOC had designed a new method of showing the service number on its B type buses. The round number plate that had been used hitherto was replaced by a number cut out in stencil which was fitted into a box let into the front of the roof of the driver's canopy. It was illuminated, and this same light also shone onto the route board. Tilling designed a similar box for its TTA1 buses except that the number box was fitted to the top of the canopy, whereas the General one came below it. Another route number box was fitted at the rear on the nearside bulkhead, and also provided a light at the back of the bus. Route 47 was the last route to carry the old style of numbering, as new TTA1s started to arrive with the modified display, and soon the older vehicles were updated also.

There was a gap in developments until early November when more new buses were added to the fleet. During that month, nine more buses were put on route 47, of which two had been taken from route 39 which was reduced to eight buses, the 47 total becoming 24.

Saturday 14th September 1912 was the last day that the horse bus service worked between Blackheath and Penge, being replaced the next day by new route 75 which worked between Woolwich (Free Ferry) and South Croydon. It used 12 motor buses including four taken from route 47, and during the next three months another eight buses were added, making a total of 20 — all from Lewisham garage which then had 50 buses plus spares.

The first two months of 1913 provided Tilling with an opportunity of preparing for the next route change by building and licensing a further batch of new buses and training the necessary men to drive them. Therefore on 2nd March 1913, 30 horse buses were withdrawn from the Dulwich (Plough) and Liverpool Street route and replaced the next day by 20 new TTA1 buses on a new motor route numbered 78, between Dulwich (Grove Tavern) and Shoreditch. These buses were allocated to Victory Place, thus doubling the fleet at that garage.

One week later on Sunday 9th March, another new route was introduced which, at first, was un-numbered. It used four motors, and extended from Bromley into the Kent countryside at Farnborough. Five weeks later when the route had become established, the logical move was made to join it to route 47, so that from 13th April service 47 ran from Shoreditch to Farnborough using 26 buses. Two weeks later a couple more buses were

New TTA1 buses were put on to the 47 route when it started on 20th July 1912. This was an extension of the Bromley and Lewisham motor route to Shoreditch via Deptford and Liverpool Street, absorbing the Lewisham and City horse bus service.

The 75 was a new service started on 15th December 1912 between South Croydon and Woolwich and it absorbed the Blackheath and Penge horse bus service. This picture of LF 9416 standing outside the 'Red Deer' at Croydon shows the new illuminated stencil box for the route number introduced in mid-1912.

Two TTA1 buses, LE 9022 and LC 4144, with a third one behind are standing outside the 'George and Dragon' at Farnborough awaiting the return trip to Shoreditch in this peaceful pre-First World War scene.

added, and at the same time two more were added to route 75 bringing its total to 22. Thus, by 27th April 1913, Tilling had licensed a total of 116 TTA1 buses for a maximum of 100 duties on six routes, three of which were joint with LGOC. Forty buses worked from Victory Place and 60 from Lewisham garage. The balance of 16 were needed to cover for breakdowns, regular overhauls, and were also used for private hire work when required.

Still with an eye to future development, more of the successful TTA1 petrol-electrics were constructed and licensed and another bus garage was needed, so in June 1913 one was opened at Acorn Street. This was just off Southampton Way with easy access to either Camberwell Road or Peckham Road. Acorn Street itself later became part of Benhill Road. Twenty-two new buses plus two spares were immediately allocated to take over operation of three adjacent routes, six buses on route 36 and eight on route 39, both from Lewisham garage, and eight from the total on route 78, making this service jointly worked with Victory Place. This change then made room for the introduction of yet another new route, the 55 running from Shoreditch to South Croydon via Deptford, Brockley, Forest Hill and Sydenham. It replaced a horse bus route between Forest Hill and Penge and required 26 buses, 14 from Lewisham and 12 from Victory Place. It was necessary to reduce the Tilling contribution on route 12 to ten buses (previously 16) but LGOC made good the shortfall.

On 7th July, more route changes took place. Tilling commenced a new and short service 92 which worked between Lewisham and Shooters Hill with four buses from Lewisham, and route 12 was extended from Peckham Rye to Nunhead. Following an exchange of duties General placed ten buses from their Old Kent Road garage on route 78, and Tilling got its first workings northeastward when it put ten buses from Victory Place on route 10 (Elephant and Castle to Wanstead). LGOC also operated B types from their Forest Gate garage (G).

As joint operation became more common, some changes in method were also necessary. Early in 1913 a new agreement between Thomas Tilling and the General provided amongst other things, that the supervision of Tilling's motor buses should pass to LGOC, who would submit a charge for this and other specified services on a mileage basis. This arrangement prevented overlapping and saved money, for previously General and Tilling inspectors could be seen side by side supervising joint routes or roads covered by the buses of both companies. Accordingly, Tilling's road staff were transferred to the General.

With joint working on routes 10 and 78, Tilling were obliged to change from their 'double shift system' to the 'block system' favoured by General. Ten days after the 7th July changes, the block system was started on the other joint routes, the 36 and 39. The block system had

A rear view of LE 9414 taken in Croydon when working the 55 route to Shoreditch, a route which was a First World War casualty. A unique feature of this service was the use of Florence Road between Deptford and Brockley, which has not been served subsequently.

begun for the ten Tilling buses on route 12 when the route was extended to Nunhead, but a return to the double shift system took place from 4th September. The reason for this was a compromise to accommodate some of Tilling's longer serving busmen; it is not known how long the old pattern continued on the 12 but it was eventually eliminated.

Some explanation of the double shift and block systems will be useful. Originally Tilling's motors on the 'Times' route were scheduled to work 12 journeys per day, and this was covered by the double shift system per bus, whereby two crews would work the early or late six journey shifts. A refreshment interval was created by widening the service slightly at the appropriate time in a slack period, when the bus would run into the Bull Yard; at other times, the buses simply turned round at the terminal for another journey. The block system was favoured by LGOC, whereby the crews worked on two different buses to build up an adequate meal interval in the gap created by transfer from the first bus to the second. On joint services, LGOC prepared the duty sheets for both companies, and thus Tilling crews had to conform to the block system. They did not, however, like the system for two main reasons. Although buses were supposed to be standardised, each one had its peculiarities which a regular driver would be familiar with. Thus, on the Tilling system a man stuck to his own bus, working early and late turns changing over

weekly and rotating through the schedule times but always with the same vehicle. Tilling found this method helped them in their record keeping and maintained efficiency, especially as a crew would be more likely to take care of their own vehicle. The second objection, by the Tilling men, was the introduction of a middle shift. At first with the implementation of the block system, it was possible to pick out the early and late duties giving them to the men with long service, whilst the spare and new men worked the middle shift. However, it still meant working on two buses. As time went on and joint working became more complicated, it was not possible for Tilling to maintain even this degree of flexibility, so they eventually capitulated to the block system, although not without a good deal of unrest and, indeed, a two-day strike.

One other aspect of the closer co-operation between LGOC and Tilling was that the Sundays favoured by Tilling for route changes had to be abandoned. The day was replaced by either a Monday or a Thursday, favoured by General at that time.

After Tilling had reduced its quota on route 39 to eight buses, LGOC had to use 16 buses to maintain the service between Sidcup and Victoria. Then, on 17th July 1913, they increased the number to 22, and the service was extended to West Kensington via Buckingham Palace Road and Brompton Road. The weekday frequency was every eight minutes and a little less on Sunday when

Tilling used their buses on route 64, but even so the Peckham to Sidcup section was also covered by Tilling Sunday route 63. Three months later on 16th October, route 39 was diverted at Victoria Station via Hyde Park Corner to run to West Kilburn over the same route as 36 serving Paddington Station and Harrow Road. It was also joined by route 39A which operated between West Kilburn and Grove Park on a 16-minute headway using B type buses from Willesden garage (AC) in the green livery of the Metropolitan Steam Omnibus Company. The eight Tillings and eight Generals on route 39 provided a similar 16-minute headway, resulting in a combined frequency of eight minutes over the common section of route between West Kilburn and Lee Green. Finally from 18th December 1913, the 39 was diverted via Edgware Road and Shirland Road instead of Harrow Road, replacing General's 51 and 51A routes over this section. These had been working between West Kilburn and either Barking or Barkingside.

Meanwhile, on 11th September, the Herne Hill and Tower Bridge horse bus service was taken off, being partly covered by four buses from Acorn Street being put on to a new short route numbered 60 between Herne Hill (Half Moon Hotel) and Peckham Rye. Five weeks later on 23rd October, 16 new buses were added and route 60 was extended from Peckham to Wood Green (Perth Road) via Trafalgar Road, Old Kent Road, London Bridge and Holloway Road. Route 78 was diverted to run via Peckham Park Road instead of Trafalgar Road. The LGOC joined in the operation of this route from 22nd January 1914, operating ten B type buses from Palmers Green garage (AD) and the Tilling quota was reduced by two, which were added to the 78 allocation.

The agreement between Thomas Tilling Ltd and LGOC which came into force on 6th October 1913 was the most far-reaching and significant. It tidied up all the previous arrangements and also set out the conditions that remained for the next 20 years. Although Tilling maintained a nominal degree of independence, there can be no doubt that LGOC dominated, and Tilling had to accept a severe amount of circumscription for the benevolent protection of the larger company. The agreement to limit the motor bus fleet to 150 buses was rigidly enforced just as Tilling were within a short distance of reaching or surpassing the total. The restriction applied within an area contained by a 30-mile radius from Charing Cross. LGOC had the power to fix routes, timetables and fares for all joint services, and they could also provide between one half and three-quarters of all buses on routes which had been exclusively Tilling's. Various methods of sharing receipts were considered, but Tilling elected to go for a pooling arrangement, which came into force from 2nd April 1914. Tilling also had to agree to give up working from its garages at Lewisham, Victory Place and Acorn Street, and to occupy LGOC premises instead, although the outbreak of the War delayed this. The restrictions contained in this agreement were so severe from Tilling's point of view that the company started to consider operations farther afield and these eventually started in Folkestone and Brighton.

A scene inside Tilling's Victory Place garage showing part of LH 8724, a petrol-electric lorry of the TTB1 type allocated to the garage for general duties. Each garage had at least one lorry.

On Sunday 19th October 1913, Sunday service 64 (Oxford Street to Bromley) was discontinued, and the 14 buses were then shared between routes 36 and 39 as on weekdays. Early the next year, on 11th January, Sunday route 63 (Oxford Circus to Sidcup) was withdrawn, and the ten Tilling buses then ran on route 12 as they did on weekdays. From June of 1913, LGOC had helped out with six B types on route 63, since Tilling's weekday allocation on route 12 had reduced from 16 to ten, and there were not enough spare for a full Tilling Sunday allocation.

In view of the terms of the October agreement with LGOC, and following the allocation to route 60 later that month, only eight new buses remained to be licensed before the total of 150 was reached. These eight were delivered in November 1913 and they entered service on an established LGOC route, the 35A (Camberwell Green to Walthamstow, Wood Street). Four buses entered service on 13th November, and another four on 27th November. The General worked the route from Leyton Green (T), Tilling from Acorn Street.

The continued competition from the growing fleet of the National Steam Car Company Ltd caused LGOC much concern, and this led to consultations which were eventually concluded from LGOC's point of view most satisfactorily, with the signing of an agreement effective from 1st January 1914 similar to that with Tilling. The National buses would work in conjunction with LGOC who would fix the routes, schedules and fares, and there would be pooling of receipts on all shared or competing routes. At that time, National ran approximately 180 buses in London from two garages, Nunhead and Putney Bridge, working on seven routes. These routes were integrated into the LGOC system and given route numbers. Starting on 12th January 1914, route 12 was revised with the three companies working in conjunction as follows:

12 Turnham Green and Nunhead 'Waverley Arms' — LGOC B types plus ten Tilling TTA1s.
12A Shepherds Bush and Peckham Rye 'Kings Arms' — National Steam Car buses.
12B Turnham Green and Brockley — LGOC B types.

From the same date the six Tilling buses were taken off route 36, leaving it entirely to LGOC, and put onto route 35A, increasing its total of petrol-electrics to 14.

TTA1 No. 165 (LE 9657) on route 55 (Shoreditch to South Croydon) was involved in a spectacular accident on Tuesday 14th May 1914 when it overturned at Penge. This happened at the Triangle by the cross road with Penge Lane and Maple Road when the bus was in collision with a Carter Paterson delivery van and overturned. The six passengers on the top deck were shot onto the pavement, and there were four more inside in addition to the conductor, driver and an inspector. Only two were seriously hurt but it served to show the seriousness of potential accidents with motor buses and increasing traffic. In practice, skidding on wet surfaces was a most common feature of early solid tyred motor buses.

Although 29th March 1914 was a date of important changes on many of London's bus routes, only two of Tilling's routes were affected. The ten buses on route 10 were moved to a new daily operation on 10A (Elephant and Castle to Buckhurst Hill). A new General route 21A replaced route 60 to Wood Green (Perth Road), the latter being diverted to South Tottenham (Cornwall Road). By this time, the LGOC were operating from Tottenham garage (AR) with Gearless Daimlers. The changes made on 23rd April 1914 had more effect on Tilling operation. Both Tilling and LGOC withdrew from routes 12 and 12B, leaving the services to the National Steam Car Company who operated as follows:

12 Shepherds Bush (White Horse) to Peckham Rye (Kings Arms)
12A Shepherds Bush (White Horse) to Dulwich (The Plough)

The General extended their number 20 route from Shepherds Bush to Turnham Green, whilst Tilling covered the former 'Times' route between Oxford Circus and Peckham and on to Brockley Station by a new route 63 which required 24 buses. Eighteen of these came from Victory Place consisting of the ten from route 12, plus eight from route 47. Six buses came from Acorn Street which were made available by a reduction of two from route 35A and four off the 60. It was under the terms of the pooling agreement with the LGOC which came into force on 2nd April 1914 that the eight Tillings taken off route 47 were replaced by a similar number of General B type buses from Dalston garage (D); thus LGOC penetrated a former Tilling preserve.

A serious accident occurred at Penge on 12th May 1914 when TTA1 No. 165 (LE 9657) collided with a Carter Patterson van and overturned. Fortunately only two passengers were hurt. It was working on route 55.

Although Tilling had now attained its maximum London fleet, LGOC continued to develop their services, and on 22nd June 1914 they extended the 21A (Wood Green to Lewisham) to Shooters Hill, thus absorbing Tilling's short 92 service. The four redundant TTA1s were added to the 75 allocation, making a total of 26. At the same time, General extended route 36 from Catford to Hither Green Station using buses from their new garage at Catford (AN), which also provided buses for the 21A.

A week later on 29th June route 60 was withdrawn, being replaced between Herne Hill and Peckham by an extension of LGOC route 37, and also by service 43A (Highgate and London Bridge) which was extended southward to Peckham Rye. Eight Tilling buses joined LGOC in working the latter route, which operated from Muswell Hill on Saturdays and Sundays. The other six Tillings spare from former route 60 were put on another established LGOC route, namely the 42 (Camberwell Green and Finsbury Park Station). The last route change before the outbreak of the First World War took place on 9th July 1914 when service 63 was extended from Brockley to Catford by way of Adelaide Road, Lewisham High Street and Rushey Green.

SUMMARY FOR 4th AUGUST 1914

Route		Garage	Buses	Joint
10A	Elephant and Castle – Buckhurst Hill	Victory Place	10	with G
35A	Camberwell Green – Walthamstow (Wood Street)	Acorn Street	12	with T
39	Sidcup (Black Horse) – West Kilburn	Acorn Street	8	with P
42	Camberwell Green – Finsbury Park Station	Acorn Street	6	with J
43A	Muswell Hill (Sat/Sun) – Highgate – Peckham Rye	Acorn Street	8	with J
47	Farnborough (George & Dragon) – Shoreditch Church	Lewisham	20	with D
55	Shoreditch Church – South Croydon (Swan & Sugar Loaf)	Lewisham	14	—
		Victory Place	12	—
63	Catford (Town Hall) – Brockley – Oxford Circus	Victory Place	18	—
		Acorn Street	6	
75	Woolwich (Free Ferry) – South Croydon (Red Deer)	Lewisham	26	—
78	Shoreditch Church – Dulwich (Grove Tavern)	Acorn Street	10	with P

Part of a line up of TTA1 buses taken from various routes operated from Acorn Street garage, engaged on a special hospital or charity outing. Buses from routes 35A, 78 and 42 are seen. By 1914 when this picture was taken, the front registration numbers had been moved to a position under the route number instead of in front of the bonnet.

3 The First World War Years 1914-1918

The outbreak of the First World War on 4th August 1914 had a dramatic effect on London's bus services, particularly with the large fleet of the LGOC. Many of the busmen were territorials or reservists and were immediately called up for war service. Within 48 hours of the outbreak of war, buses were commandeered off the streets for home troop movement, and single-deckers were requisitioned for the Admiralty medical service. During September the famous B types and MET Daimlers were being commandeered for troop movements abroad, especially in Belgium, and on October 12th three hundred buses were demanded by the War Office. Altogether, some 1,319 were taken for war service. The War Office did not take any of Tilling's petrol-electrics nor any of National's steam buses, but LGOC's dire straits had repercussions on other companies within the London Pool. Many bus routes were reduced, altered or withdrawn, and Tilling operation was revised to cover some of these losses. To some extent south east London was fortunate in having a number of tram routes to compensate. Seven of LGOC's bus garages were also requisitioned, including those at Catford (AN) and Camberwell (Q) in Tilling territory.

The first changes took place on 13th August 1914 when LGOC withdrew service 21A, and the short route 92 was reinstated between Lewisham and Shooters Hill, covered by four Tilling buses that had been allocated to route 75. Service 43A was also reduced so that the eight Tilling buses were taken off in order to increase the number of TTA1s on route 42 to fourteen, which represented half the total allocation for that route. Route 43A was withdrawn between London Bridge and Peckham Rye on Sundays from 25th October 1914 and on weekdays from 7th December 1914.

The closure of Camberwell garage caused a large reorganisation of Tilling's services from 2nd November 1914. The War Office needed the garage, as well as several others, for use as a depot for motor transport. Tilling's most recent services (the 55 and 63) were withdrawn entirely, so providing a stock of vehicles to replace certain General services. Twelve buses from Acorn Street were put on route 37 (Peckham High Street) to Isleworth (Market Place), and 14 from Victory Place went on to route 40 (Elephant and Castle to Upton Park). Tilling also regained full operation on two of its original routes, the 47 and 78. Ten extra TTA1s were put onto the 78 whilst in the case of the 47, there was some reduction in mileage as only 18 buses ran the full route from Shoreditch to Farnborough, and 16 buses ran a short working between Shoreditch and Bromley Common (The Crown) numbered 47A. Operation on the 10 group of routes was revised, and the Tilling buses moved from 10A to 10B (Elephant and Castle to Wanstead via Forest Gate) as 12 buses were able to

work the entire route. However this did not last long, for on 30th November the 10B was withdrawn and the 40 extended to Wanstead as 40A, a route which Tilling operated with 11 buses. Tilling then resumed work on the 10A to Buckhurst Hill with 13 buses. On the same day, Tilling took a greater share on route 35A, increasing to 20 buses by using four from route 78 and three from the 40. Two extra buses working from Acorn Street took Tilling's maximum service buses to 152, two above the agreement, but in the exigencies of war the LGOC were pleased to use whatever was available.

Frequent changes were made to Tilling's bus services during the war years as routes were altered or adapted to best advantage, for although Tilling had not lost any buses to the War Department, the General had a much reduced fleet.

The LGOC-operated 39A route had been withdrawn on 12th August 1914, but the joint LGOC and Tilling route 39 between Sidcup and West Kilburn lingered on for another four months until 7th December 1914 when it also was withdrawn. The section of road beyond Lewisham was covered by an extension of route 21 which ran through from Crouch End Broadway and beyond Lewisham to Sidcup. It was worked by ten B types from Palmers Green garage and 13 TTA1s from Lewisham garage. Eight of these had been made redundant by the withdrawal of the 39, and four came off route 92 which again disappeared, being covered by the return of the 21A working between Crouch End and Shooters Hill.

On January 25th 1915, LGOC lost another garage to the War Office when Catford (AN) was closed and taken over for military transport purposes. It had been opened as recently as the spring of 1914. It operated buses on routes 21, 36 and 47, and buses also worked on a 61 (Greenwich and Sidcup) and 136 (Bromley and Westerham Hill). Some single deckers also operated from this garage on routes 112 (Penge and Bromley) and 113 (Beckenham and Park Langley). It became a branch of the central depot of the Royal Army Service Corps at Grove Park. Some of its duties were taken over by Tilling, who gave up operation on 10A and 40A. This enabled 11 TTA1s to work on the 21A (Crouch End and Shooters Hill) and 12 on the 36 (West Kilburn and Hither Green Station). The return of Tilling to the 36 in particular seemed like a homecoming after an absence of about a year, and Tilling buses returned to West Kilburn once more only a few weeks after they had been withdrawn from that area with the loss of route 39. As two additional buses were put onto the 35A at the same time, the maximum number of Tilling buses in service rose to 154. This was not to last for long as on 18th March 1915 it went down to 150 when four TTA1s were sent to Brighton. Tilling had been seeking business elsewhere and Hove Council had granted 12 licences to operate in the area. In the event only five of the licences were taken and five buses sent to Sussex, the four mentioned plus one from spares at Acorn Street.

It is worth mentioning that the agreement to limit the operating fleet to 150 applied to weekdays only, and at various times the Sunday total exceeded this. In the summer of 1915, extra Sunday buses were operated: four more buses ran on route 75 and two more each on routes 42, 47 and 78.

The summer season of 1915, commencing in May, saw the return of the full service to Farnborough on route 47 and the withdrawal of the 47A, but the route returned from 22nd November 1915 and continued the winter pattern until 15th May 1916. From 17th June 1915, certain buses on route 21 (duty numbers 9 to 13) began working beyond Sidcup to Foots Cray during the morning and also the evening and night to carry war workers to the various munitions factories in the area. In order to save petrol and reduce mileage, it was necessary from 8th July to cut back both services 21 and 21A from Crouch End at the northern end to terminate at Wood Green (Wellington).

One of the most serious demands of the war was the need of the armed forces for more and more men, and the employment situation in the bus industry became serious. The logical answer was the employment of women as bus conductors but this solution came very slowly. The trade unions were suspicious until they were reassured that such employment would be strictly temporary and at the male rates of pay. The LGOC still hesitated before giving their approval for women conductors, who eventually began work in March 1916, but Tilling's first woman conductor appeared earlier, on 1st November 1915 on a 37 bus from Acorn Street garage. Before long a number of women were employed in this capacity. There were problems with the issuing of suitable uniforms for summer and winter and with the need for toilet facilities at garages and terminal points. In January 1916, all women were transferred to the new garage at Croydon. Conductresses were employed at Croydon until 11th June 1919.

The implementation of that aspect of the agreement between Tilling and LGOC whereby Tilling gave up its garage premises and operated from accommodation provided by the General was much delayed but not shelved. The LGOC had built a new garage in London Road, Croydon and this was handed over to Tilling, who gave up using their own garage at Victory Place for buses and this was then used for commercial vehicles operated under contract by Tilling. The move took place on Saturday night 22nd January 1916 when the 40 service buses from Victory Place garage together with their crews were transferred to Lewisham garage. At the same time, 40 buses from Lewisham and four from Acorn Street were moved to the new garage at Croydon, from which three routes were operated (The 75 and 75A were jointly worked with Lewisham garage which operated ten buses on each service):

59	Camden Town and South Croydon (Sundays)	
	Oxford Circus and South Croydon (weekdays)	26 buses
75	Woolwich and South Croydon	8 buses
75A	Woolwich and South Croydon via Forest Hill	10 buses

Immediately prior to closure, Victory Place had been providing buses for four routes, 21A, 47, 47A and 78.

Photo of first woman conductress to enter Tilling service in 1915 on service 37, Peckham and Isleworth, from Acorn Street garage. Note the heavy coat, bell punch and ticket rack.

Driver and woman conductor stand in front of 78 bus LH 8675 at the 'Grove Hotel' Dulwich. The destination board on the bus reads 'Camberwell Green' indicating a return journey to Acorn Street garage.

Croydon garage, built by the LGOC, was handed over to Tilling on 23rd January 1916 and a number of TTA1 buses were transferred to it from other garages. This line-up shows the buses ready for operation on routes 59 and 75.

Buses on the 21A were replaced by ten General vehicles from Old Kent Road garage (P), and those on the 47 by 19 Generals from Dalston garage. Lewisham took over the 47A using 16 buses. Operation of the 78 was taken over entirely by Acorn Street with an extra ten buses, but Tilling operation of the 37 ceased, as Streatham (AK) garage now took on those duties. This latter garage in turn lost the 59 route to the new Croydon garage. The year 1916 heralded a period during the war when Tilling buses were used to support the General in providing coverage on certain routes which served Woolwich, so as to carry the increasingly large numbers of munition workers to Woolwich Arsenal; hence the introduction of the new 75A service. The 75 was extended on 29th May to Plumstead (Plume of Feathers) with two extra buses taken off the 21.

Wartime shortages, particularly of petrol, made bus operation very difficult during 1916. From 16th July, all extra buses were cancelled on Sundays. From 31st July, the 20 buses from Acorn Street in use on route 35A were taken off and the weekday route was suspended for a few months. The Sunday service which had been extended to Chingford on 16th April continued until 6th August using General buses. On 14th August, 16 of the surplus buses at Acorn Street were transferred to Croydon garage increasing its total to 60 buses. The

75 and 75A routes were reallocated, with Croydon working 14 on the 75 and 16 on the 75A, which meant that Lewisham's quota reduced to six and four respectively. Acorn Street put four buses on the 36, reducing the number at Lewisham, and enabling an extra 16 buses to be worked on the 47, the General buses being temporarily withdrawn. Croydon also put four more buses on route 59. On 7th August, four TTA1s were taken off route 21 and put onto a new service numbered 91 which worked between Lewisham and Shooters Hill and replaced the LGOC operated 21A service. However, General's 21A was reinstated on 18th September 1916 and the 91 was revised to operate between Brockley (Breakspeare Arms) and Plumstead (Plume of Feathers) via Lee Green and Charlton Road to Woolwich. Eight Tillings were taken off the 36 route so as to provide the 12 needed for the extended 91 and were replaced by General buses from Willesden garage (AC).

As if the war shortages were not bad enough, the months of November and December 1916 contributed some of the worst London smogs to the difficulties of operation. A considerable mileage was lost, two of the worst examples being on Saturday 16th December, nearly 7000 miles, and Wednesday 27th December, over 8000 miles.

The year 1917 was perhaps the worst of all for bus operation. The remaining four Tilling buses which had worked from Acorn Street since 14th August 1916 were taken off route 36 on 1st March 1917, leaving the route in the hands of General once more. Then on 19th March, Acorn Street garage, Camberwell, was itself closed as far as bus operation was concerned, leaving some 30 buses spare. Twenty-two of these TTA1s were then transferred to Brighton, where Thomas Tilling Ltd had in the preceding December purchased Brighton, Hove and Preston Omnibus Company. The petrol-electrics were needed so that older Brighton vehicles could be withdrawn.

Considerable reorganisation accompanied the closure of Acorn Street garage. Tilling gave up operation on route 42, and the 78 was transferred to Lewisham. Tilling ceased to work entirely on route 21, and General returned to the 47 using 14 B type buses from Dalston. Routes 75 and 75A (the latter was renumbered 72) were entirely worked from Croydon, each requiring 21 buses. Route 91 was extended to Sydenham Station via Forest Hill and acquired an extra bus, bringing the total to 13. Tilling also operated on two new routes: nine buses on a 93 which was a munitions service between Woolwich (Earl of Chatham) and Sidcup (Black Horse) — the latter terminal very familiar to Tilling busmen; and two buses on a 98 between Peckham and Honor Oak. This latter route only lasted two months, being taken off on 25th May, and Honor Oak had then to wait over two years before it saw another bus service. The 93 was a little more successful and had certain journeys projected to

Foots Cray. It was withdrawn weekdays from 13th August 1917 but the Sunday service lingered on until 21st October but worked by the LGOC. Route 91 was also withdrawn, and route 72 provided at least a part replacement diverted via Brockley and Lewisham instead of Catford and Lee Green. The Tilling buses released were redistributed as follows:

36 (West Kilburn and Hither Green) 10 buses.
36A (West Kilburn and Grove Park Station) 8 buses.
75 (Plumstead and Croydon) 4 extra buses from Lewisham.

One of the war's major effects on the periphery of Tilling's territory was the vast expansion of the Royal Arsenal at Woolwich to supply the very large quantities of munitions needed. Thousands of workers came from a large hinterland of south London and beyond to work there, and virtually all of these needed public transport. LGOC and its associates found itself hard pressed at times to carry this extra trade, especially as it suffered from the usual disadvantages of peak traffic with a sharp demand for transport, followed by periods when vehicles were hardly used at all. Thus, many buses would only be needed in the early morning and late afternoons, and this was hardly a profitable use of resources and capital. LGOC was not well endowed with garages in the area. Indeed, the only two, Catford (AN) and Plumstead (AM), had already been taken over by the War Office with consequent loss of operation. To cover these financial losses the Ministry of Munitions agreed to make a subsidy in respect of certain specified routes that carried munitions workers. This was claimed each month or

Five TTA1s are lined up outside the 'Red Deer' at South Croydon in 1917. The two routes were in use to carry munition workers to Woolwich, the 72 running via Forest Hill and Brockley and the 75 via Sydenham and Blackheath, the latter terminating at Plumstead.

quarter from July 1916 to November 1918. The following Tilling services were included during the period of the subsidy:

21 Wood Green to Foots Cray via Woolwich.
72 South Croydon to Woolwich via Eltham Hill (diverted via Lewisham, Lee Green, Blackheath and Charlton).
75 South Croydon to Plumstead via Sydenham.
75A South Croydon to Woolwich via Forest Hill (this number was later in the war used for short journeys on the 75 between Plumstead Station and Lower Sydenham).
91 Sydenham to Plumstead.
93 Woolwich to Sidcup (certain journeys extended to Foots Cray).

The number 75A was in use again from 18th March 1918 for a short working of the 75 between Plumstead Station and Lower Sydenham (Bell Green), thereby increasing the frequency over this section of the route. The 12 buses which were needed were provided by taking six from the 75 and six from the 36 and 36A. Following the cessation of hostilities the 75A was withdrawn on 30th November 1918 and the 12 buses returned to their former duties.

With the closure of the inner London garages and the opening of Croydon in January 1916, Tilling's centre of operation shifted considerably towards the central south of London and, instead of the Essex countryside, penetrated Surrey as well as Kent. From the opening of Croydon garage route 59 (South Croydon to Oxford Circus, extended to Camden Town on Sundays) was taken over from Streatham garage and at first required 26 buses. The route had originally started as a Sunday-only service, becoming daily from 12th December 1912. Since the opening of Streatham garage in 1913 it had been operated by 'B' type buses in the blue livery of the Tramways (MET) Omnibus Company with the fleetname 'M.E.T.' on the side. The green painted Daimlers of the British Automobile Company also operated on the route from their Camden Town garage between January 1913 and June 1914.

From 16th April 1916 the 59 on Sundays was split, with 18 buses working the 59 to Croydon and eight extended to Caterham as the 59A. Four months later on Monday 14th August, the 59 was divided into sections on weekdays as well, working as follows: 59 (Oxford Circus and South Croydon) every 15 minutes with 12 buses; 59A (Oxford Circus and Caterham) every 30 minutes with 8 buses; 59B (Oxford Circus and Reigate) every 30 minutes with 10 buses. The 59A and 59B replaced two General operated routes which had been 152 (Stockwell and Caterham) and 160 (Stockwell and Reigate).

During the remaining two years of war, Tilling was obliged to reduce the number of buses operating on the 59 group of routes owing to petrol restrictions and the requirement to maintain the maximum operation on the munition routes 72, 75 and 75A. To keep the total of 60 buses operating from Lewisham garage, all reductions were at the expense of Croydon. Nevertheless, regular workings every 15 minutes to Croydon and thirty minutes to Caterham, Merstham or Reigate were maintained throughout the war with the assistance of the LGOC who ran, as required, MET buses out of Streatham garage. After November 1916, the fleetname of these buses was changed to 'Metropolitan' and upon overhaul the buses were painted red.

Six buses were taken off route 59 on 1st March 1917, reducing the frequency to 30 minutes and making a joint headway of ten minutes to Croydon with 59A and 59B. This was the most difficult time of the war, and changes were frequent. Another temporary operation came into being on 19th March when the 59A and 59B were withdrawn, leaving 23 buses to work the 59. As replacements, LGOC ran two routes from Thornton Heath with buses from Streatham garage. Five buses ran on the 94 route to Caterham, and six on the 95 to Reigate. However, shortages of petrol got worse and these temporary workings ran only for a fortnight. Revised schedules on Monday 2nd April brought Tilling to its lowest ebb of the war. Nineteen buses were taken off route 59 from the previous Saturday and this reduced Tilling's service bus operation to 106 vehicles. The 59A and 59B resumed operation and, together with the 59, were extended from Oxford Circus to Camden Town daily. Four Tilling buses only ran on 59 together with nine MET buses from AK, and MET also ran the 59A and 59B with nine and eleven buses respectively.

Tilling having reached this low point, the position then reversed. Another six buses were put on the 59 on 10th May 1917, two more on 59A on 21st May, followed by another 14 for the 59A on 4th June, ten having been taken off the 59 which was left to MET. By the 13th August, Tilling was in a position to increase its wartime fleet to 120 buses, and thus 22 TTA1s ran on the 59A for the rest of the summer, giving an improved headway to Caterham of 15 minutes. With the winter schedules on 29th October, eight TTA1s were removed from the 59A and these joined the MET buses on the 59 route. These eight buses moved to the 59B on 29th November, the route being cut back to Coulsdon. MET worked the 59 and helped with 59B, which was extended to Merstham on 29th March 1918. The position then stabilised for the rest of the war. Eventually, Monday 11th November 1918 dawned and at 11am on that day the Armistice was signed that ended the hostilities of the First World War.

SUMMARY FOR 11th NOVEMBER 1918

Route	Detail	Garage	Buses	Joint
36	West Kilburn – Hither Green	Lewisham	6	with AC
36A	West Kilburn – Grove Park	Lewisham	8	with AC
47	Shoreditch Church – Farnborough	Lewisham	16	with D
59A	Camden Town – Caterham	Croydon	14	—
59B	Camden Town – Merstham	Croydon	8	—
72	South Croydon 'Red Deer' – Brockley – Woolwich	Croydon	20	—
75	South Croydon – Plumstead (Church Manor Way)	Croydon	18	—
		Lewisham	2	—
75A	Lower Sydenham (Bell Green) – Plumstead (Church Manor Way)	Lewisham	12	—
78	Shoreditch Church – Dulwich 'Grove Hotel'	Lewisham	16	—

4 A Slow Recovery 1919-1923

The First World War had dealt rather harshly with the London bus. Vehicles themselves were in woefully short supply, and whereas on the day of the outbreak of the war LGOC and its associates owned a fleet of 3,071 buses, the number of buses operating on the streets on Armistice Day was 1,758. This figure rose to 1,905 by the first day of 1919. Whilst it is true that Tilling had not lost buses to the war effort as had been the case with LGOC, yet shortages and difficulties had reduced Tilling's operating service buses from the maximum of 150 to 120. Travelling by bus had become a rather uncomfortable experience, and it had been during the war that standing passengers had been permitted for the first time on the lower deck. Services and frequencies had been progressively reduced and manpower was in short supply. In south east London, Tilling also had to try to cover for the gaps with the requisition of Camberwell, Catford (AN) and Plumstead garages from the LGOC. Recovery was bound to be slow. The country might be emerging from the war as victor, but to the bus operator still short of staff, vehicles, parts and fuel, it must have seemed a pyrrhic victory. There would be no immediate return to peacetime conditions as the economy revived only slowly, and co-operation between the London bus pooling group of companies would be even more essential.

The year 1919 opened with Tilling operating 120 petrol-electric buses on the streets of London on eight routes. Sixty buses each came from Lewisham and Croydon garages. The only changes from Armistice Day had been the withdrawal on 30th November of route 75A. This allowed both routes 36 and 36A to operate ten

buses apiece from Lewisham, with eight and six buses respectively provided by General from their Willesden garage. Also, six extra buses were put on to the 75. Tilling continued to work the longer route 47, whilst Dalston provided 14 B types for the 47A. Tilling's three exclusive routes remained the 72, 75 and 78. At Croydon, Tilling provided 14 buses for 59A and eight for 59B, leaving LGOC to provide 20 buses from Streatham (AK) for the 59 and also a share to the 59B which were usually B types in the MET livery. The 59A ran every 20 minutes to Caterham, while the 59B had a 40-minute frequency to Merstham. This changed, however, on 10th February 1919 when LGOC took over the 59B, providing a bus every half hour, and eight Tilling buses joined General in operating the 59 service.

Following the cessation of hostilities, the need to serve Woolwich Arsenal reduced, and the government subsidy for certain services was withdrawn. This led to a change in the pattern of the routes in the area when, on 21st May 1919, route 72 was withdrawn between Woolwich and Lewisham and diverted to Shoreditch via Deptford and London Bridge. It is interesting to note that this route had already been covering the roads of the pre-war 55 between Croydon, Forest Hill and Brockley, and with one exception it now covered the roads right through to Shoreditch Church. Coming southwards, the 55 had turned right into Deptford Broadway and then into Florence Road (a road not used by buses subsequently) and into Shardeloes Road to reach Brockley, whereas the 72 ran on to Lewisham via the 47 and then via Ladywell and Adelaide Road to reach Brockley in the same way as pre-war route 63.

An inspector and woman conductor are seen standing by a 36A bus at the Grove Park terminus, no doubt soon after the route commenced operation from West Kilburn in August 1917. A brass letter 'L' is seen under the running number, indicating that the bus is from Lewisham garage.

It was now the turn of the 36 family to respond to increasing demand. On 10th February 1919 the 36 was given an improved headway which required a total of 28 buses, 14 each from Tilling and General. The 36A was diverted at Edgware Road and sent on to Kilburn Station instead of West Kilburn, which required six Tilling buses and nine Generals from Cricklewood garage (W). This was shortlived, for three months later on 7th May, 36A was renumbered 39 and extended to North Finchley (Swan and Pyramids) via Edgware Road and Golders Green. LGOC added an extra five buses to cover this extension. This 39 ran to Grove Park Station along the same roads as 36A had done by way of Catford jointly with 36, and then along Newstead Road. The service had a 15-minute frequency and from end to end the journey time was 135 minutes. Four months later on 3rd September, there was another alteration when the 39 was withdrawn between North Finchley and Golders Green, and projected to Hendon (Bell). In the south, it was withdrawn between Catford and Grove Park, and instead was extended through Bromley to Farnborough (George and Dragon). This slightly longer route maintained its 15-minute frequency, but as it worked so much in Tilling territory its operation was left entirely to that company, using 22 buses. This meant readjustment, so 16 buses were taken from route 78 to add to the six already on the 39. General now took over operation of route 78 using B type buses from its recently reopened Camberwell garage upon its return from the War Department. A replacement 36A was introduced at the same time between Grove Park and West Kilburn via Catford, only now it was worked entirely by LGOC using buses from Willesden and Camberwell garages.

The overlong 39 was apparently not a success, although it speaks well for the reliability of the TTA1 that such a route could be operated at all. It only lasted for just over three months and was withdrawn on 10th December. The buses made spare were divided: five went onto the 36, reducing the General's total, and 17 onto the 36A, which then became entirely Tilling operated. A Sunday variation of the 36 resulted in an extension from West Kilburn to Willesden from 7th September, but it only lasted until Sunday 22nd February 1920.

Mention has already been made of the reduction in Tilling's working fleet from the permitted maximum of 150 to a wartime total of 120 buses. The reductions commenced in March 1917, all being made with the Croydon fleet. After the cessation of hostilities in November 1918, London's bus fleets took some months to get back to normal. Many difficulties occurred and it took time to add to the depleted fleets of vehicles and also to engage new staff, even though many men were coming back from war service. Many women conductors were still being employed but the last of them were paid off at Croydon garage on 11th June 1919. It was June 1919 before Tilling's bus fleet could be increased and during that month and early July six additional buses were put on to route 75 from Croydon garage. By 1st September four extra buses were allocated to the 59A route. The additional buses were all TTA1 type that had been in store. Between 7th May and 2nd December 1919, route 59 on weekdays was extended from Croydon to Kenley, supporting the 59A over that section of road; it needed 24 buses, eight Tillings and 16 Generals. The 59B was extended to Reigate on Sundays during the summer months.

Three additions to the fleet on 3rd December 1919, placed on the 59A service, were reported as 'new' buses. They appeared to have the TTA2 type of chassis with standard bonnet and Tilling-style fluted radiator with the legend 'TILLING-STEVENS' at the top, but with a flat-bottomed base without the words 'Petrol-Electric' familiar with the TS3 and later types. They carried 34-seat bodies and registration numbers from former TTA1 class vehicles. Undoubtedly they were not new buses but were built from spare TTA2 chassis (maybe former lorries) and stored TTA1 bodies.

Until this time, an average of 52-55 buses had been working the 59 group of routes, with some 30 LGOC buses running out of Streatham garage, currently on 59 and 59B, and Tilling's buses on 59 and 59A. Between December 1919 and March 1920, the number of General buses on the routes declined, as Tilling was able to bring back more buses into use; by 31st March 1920, fifteen extra Tilling buses had been added to the group. Ten of these, however, were taken from route 72 and replaced

In December 1919 a few Tilling buses were introduced that had been built from spare TTA2 chassis previously in use as lorries. They had the later style of Tilling-Stevens bonnet and former TTA1 bodies and registration numbers. LF 9843 is standing at the 'Red Deer' at Croydon, on the 72 route, which by that time was working to Shoreditch instead of Woolwich.

by ten LGOC B types from Clay Hall (Y) garage, and this was the only time that the General ever worked on either the 72 or 75. For the first time since 1916, the 59 was worked entirely by Tilling buses from Croydon garage. There were 22 on route 59 to Croydon, 18 on the 59A to Caterham and 11 on the 59B to Merstham, which was extended to Reigate on Sundays during the summer months.

Allocations changed frequently that summer. On 9th June 1920, ten buses were taken off the 59 and put on to the 59B, giving an improved service on that long route. Two months later on 11th August, ten Tilling buses were put back onto route 72, and the Generals were withdrawn. As a direct result, Streatham had to return to the 59 group with ten buses to make up the loss; they were split as follows: two on the 59, three on the 59A and five on the 59B. Passengers must have wondered what type of bus they would find on their local route — TTA1 or TTA2 Tilling or B type in General or MET livery, but all were of standard size with 34-seat bodies and open tops. With the introduction of winter schedules on 10th November 1920, the 59B was reduced to 11 vehicles once more, and the B types were only to be found on the 59. Another change during the summer of 1920 was that for the period from 23rd May to 3rd October, route 59 was withdrawn on Sundays, and 13 buses were put onto route 152, which ran from Stockwell to Caterham. Over the same period, Metropolitan B types worked route 160 between Stockwell and Reigate. These two routes were both revivals of four years previously when they last ran. It was unusual for routes to return after such a long gap without at least having altered their number.

The bus garage which the General had built in Bromley Road, Catford and opened in 1914 had been closed in January 1915 when it was taken over by the War Department, but it was released late in 1920. General then handed the garage over to Tilling, which was able to transfer its buses from Lewisham garage with its limited accommodation. On Saturday 2nd October 1920, the 62 TTA1 buses on routes 36, 36A, 47 and 75 came out of Lewisham in the morning and ran into Catford in the evening.

On 20th November 1920 the headquarters of Thomas Tilling was changed from Winchester House, Peckham to 20 Victoria Street, Westminster as it had become less of a local concern. The limitation in the number of buses which could be operated in London had caused the company to move into the provinces, first to Folkestone in 1914, to Brighton in 1916 and to Ipswich in 1919.

The practice of Tilling buses carrying a duty number appears to have started about 1909 when they were first operated in conjunction with LGOC. This was, no doubt, so that inspectors could check on timekeeping. The numbers were shown on a small enamel plate fixed in slots on the side of the bus — in the case of the TTA1, the slots were to be found on the sides of the driver's seat. At a later date, probably in 1916, a small brass letter was put on the sides of the bus near to the duty number indicating to which garage the bus was allocated, namely 'C' for Croydon and 'L' for Lewisham. The letter 'L' was transferred to the new Catford garage when it opened. In about April 1924 these garage codes were revised to TC and TL, thus avoiding confusion with General's C and L garages.

The larger capacity of Catford garage enabled a degree of rationalisation to take place whereby ten buses on route 72 could be transferred to Catford from Croydon, on 24th November, thus improving the efficiency of the route's operation. Gradually during 1919-1921, Tilling's working fleet crept back up to the 150 buses of the pre-war agreement. Mention has already been made of the 17 extra buses added to the Croydon fleet, and the fleet at Lewisham had been increased by two extra buses put onto the 36. By 31st March 1920, Tilling buses in service totalled 139. Then on 16th December 1920, two more appeared on route 59 with one more in January and two in March 1921. These were TTA1s returning to London service at Croydon. On 27th April 1921, two more new buses were put on to 59B, being of the TTA2 type with TTA1 bodies and registrations. It is not known how many of these rebuilds there were in all, but Mr Webb mentions five specifically and the number was certainly not very large.

A short-lived variation of the 36 route took place from 19th January 1921 when it was amalgamated with the

The TTA1 type of bus continued to operate on the 47 route until early 1922. As this picture shows, a reduction in route details on the sides of the bus had taken place by this time, the route number alone being carried on the upper deck rail. Route details are shown on the board below the lower deck windows. A similar change had taken place with General B type buses.

36A, giving a total of 36 buses. Grove Park was served by certain journeys continuing on to that point instead of terminating at Hither Green. This was a weekday-only operation. From 22nd March, the Grove Park journeys ceased and from the next day a revised 36A came into operation, running from Camden Town Station via Albert Road and serving the Zoo and Baker Street, and then via the 36 from Marble Arch to Lewisham. The 36A then went via Lee Green and Burnt Ash Road to terminate at Grove Park, a routeing reminiscent of the pre-war 39A. This 36A was operated by LGOC using 16 buses from Chalk Farm (CF) garage. Tilling buses came on to the 36A again on 8th June when eight buses were taken off route 36 and joined eight General buses in working the route, Chalk Farm being replaced by Camberwell at that time.

On 16th February, route 75 was extended from Woolwich to Abbey Wood in order to replace a section of LGOC's route 48 (Paddington Green and Abbey Wood). Four extra buses were needed, and came off the 59. Two more buses were also removed from route 59, and added to the total for route 72 on 23rd March, when it was withdrawn between London Bridge and Shoreditch and extended to Charing Cross via Fleet Street and Strand. On 4th August, bus number 213 hit the headlines whilst working on this route when it skidded and crashed into a wall at Brockley Rise, killing the driver.

The TTA1 type of bus was long overdue for replacement; it had served the company well, but many were showing signs of wear, and the LGOC had already in service a sizeable number of a larger bus, the K type with a 46-seat body. However, a larger type of bus was eventually designed using the Tilling-Stevens TS3A chassis, for which a 48-seat body was built at Tilling's own workshops. It had a wider body permitting forward-facing seats on the lower deck, which was a great advantage over the longitudinal seating of the older type. This type of body became standard for the remainder of the petrol-electric era. With this new class of vehicle came a change in the style of fleetname shown on the vehicles. The TTA1s always had 'THOS TILLING LTD' in capital letters on the sides of the bus. On the TS3As, this was altered to script lettering in gold on a centre panel painted white reading 'Thomas Tilling Limited' with the word 'Tilling' being larger than the other words.

The prototype, numbered 805 and carrying registration XB 9960, entered service from Croydon garage on route 59B on 9th July 1921. The second new bus followed on 20th August, and this brought Tilling's working fleet to 148 buses; on 17th August, two spare TTA1s were added to route 59, bringing the total back to 150. This was divided between the two garages, 72 at Catford, and 78 at Croydon. The third TS3A entered service on 20th August and was put to work on the 59B, and between September and October another 11 new buses were licensed and put on this same route. The replacement programme for the pre-war buses was starting to get under way.

Winter schedules were introduced on Wednesday 19th October 1921, and this resulted in a revision to the 59 group of services so that the 46 Tilling buses were redistributed as follows: 59 (Camden Town and Croydon, diverted to Thornton Heath) 12 buses; 59A (Camden Town and Caterham, instead of Godstone) 19 buses; 59B (Camden Town and Coulsdon, instead of Reigate) 15 buses.

Delivery of new vehicles continued and when on 2nd November another new bus arrived it was put on to the 59B, thus completing the 15 new TS3As for the route. On the same day the first two of the new TS3A buses were sent to Catford garage for use on the 36. The next two new buses sent to Croydon were placed on the 59A. Between the beginning of November 1921 and the middle of January 1922, 40 new TS3As had been delivered, being sent either to Croydon or Catford garages to replace the older TTA1 vehicles. The new Catford buses went on to the 36 and this route was nearly complete. The extra 17 TS3As sent to Croydon provided the full allocation for the 59A service, but this was altered by a route change that took place in January 1922. Route 72, which had been working every 12 minutes between Charing Cross and South Croydon with 12 buses from Croydon and ten from Catford was withdrawn after 17th January 1922, being partly replaced the next day by other services. The route from London Bridge to Lewisham was already covered by service 47, and the section from Lewisham to Forest Hill via Brockley was replaced by a diversion of General's route 49A (Lewisham and Shepherds Bush). Part of route 12 (Shepherds Bush and Dulwich) was extended to Penge (Crooked Billet) under the number 12A, whilst a new route 68A (Chalk Farm and South Croydon) covered the remainder of the route from Norwood Junction. This really involved the breaking up of a well-established cross-suburban route, for the pre-war 55 had wound its way through the same suburban roads. Direct links had been severed between Forest Hill, Penge and Croydon and there was a public outcry. Therefore, on 8th March 1922, the 12A service was revised to work from Charing Cross instead of Shepherds Bush and extended from Penge to South Croydon (Red Deer), thereby using both terminals of the former 72 but by a mainly different route. Two weeks later on 22nd March, a more suitable terminal was found for the 12A by extending it from Charing Cross to Oxford Circus.

The 49A and 68A routes were operated entirely by General but the new 12A was to be jointly worked by Tilling and General. Therefore some rearrangement was necessary between the two companies so as to utilise the 22 Tilling buses off the 72 service. This was achieved by transferring two buses from Croydon to Catford garage and nine buses being put on to the 47 route, which thus became entirely Tilling. The nine Generals from Dalston garage were used elsewhere. Three more Tillings were put on the 36A, increasing the total to eleven and the LGOC reduced to five. Both the 36A and 47 were still being operated by the older TTA1 buses. Ten buses from Croydon garage were put on to the new 12A service, being worked jointly with nine General K type from Nunhead (AH) garage. It was decided that the smaller TTA1s would be unsuitable for this new operation and as only one new TS3A was available, nine of the new buses were taken from the 59A, which had to have some TTA1s back again. During the next few weeks, as new buses arrived they were put on to the 59A and it again had a full quota of TS3A buses. By February 1922, 48 of the new TS3A type had entered service from Croydon garage for routes 59A, 59B, and 12A. Four spares were also included. Catford had only received 34 new buses in the same time, which enabled the conversion of the 36 with 28 buses and a start to be made on the 47.

A new and improved type of petrol-electric bus was designed in 1921. Mounted on a TS3A chassis it seated forty-eight passengers and 166 of the design were built. The photos show the offside and nearside of No. 990 (XM 1409), one of the last to be delivered late in 1922. Note the fleet number on the chassis frame and the letter 'L' indicating allocation to Catford garage.

Once again with the commencement of the high summer timetables on 31st May 1922, Croydon garage saw changes. The 59B was improved so that it offered a ten-minute frequency as far as Coulsdon and 20 minutes to Reigate. This needed 27 buses. Six buses were taken off the 59A, which ran every 20 minutes to Caterham only, and a reduced frequency on the 59 provided another three buses for 59B. The other three buses came off route 75 which was withdrawn between Abbey Wood and Woolwich. The 59B needed the new TS3A type, whilst the 75 was still worked by TTA1s. Consequently, six new buses which had just entered service on the 59 passed to the Reigate route and some older buses returned once more to the 59, although this only lasted for a few weeks before new buses re-appeared on the Thornton Heath working.

The 47 route was also subject to change between the summer and the winter. It will be recalled that during the winter period from October to May, alternate buses terminated at Bromley Common (Crown) and were numbered 47A, but with the onset of high summer in May, all buses continued through to Farnborough and the 47A was withdrawn. New TS3A buses continued to arrive during the summer and autumn of 1922 and enabled the conversion of the 47 (and 47A when it returned in October) and a start to be made on the 36A. Croydon was converting the 59 and 75 simultaneously.

On 7th September 1921, the LGOC had introduced a new bus service between Lewisham and Elmers End numbered 71. It was operated by five 26-seat B type single deckers from Old Kent Road garage. The route was extended through to South Croydon (Swan and Sugar Loaf) on 12th April 1922, and by agreement was handed over to Tilling to operate from Croydon garage.

The same five B types plus one spare were loaned to Tilling for this operation. Although the route had almost doubled in length, the same number of vehicles were operated and so the frequency widened from 15 to 30 minutes. This lasted just six months, as following a revision of routes on 11th October 1922, the 71 was withdrawn and route 54A (previously Camden Town and Forest Hill) was changed to work between Charing Cross and South Croydon at a 15-minute frequency. This was worked by 16 Tilling buses of TS3A type, achieved by six Catford buses being taken off the 36A and ten buses from Croydon, seven removed from the 59B (reduced service for the winter season) and three from the 59. As replacements, the LGOC put six buses on the 36A from Old Kent Road, and five from Norwood on the 59. Trunk route 54 (Charing Cross and Keston) remained exclusively the preserve of the General.

By the middle of October 1922 only about 16 of the TS3As on order remained outstanding and on 19th December the last one was licensed, which made 166 in total. The remaining TTA1s were withdrawn and either sold or scrapped. The last in service had worked route 75 from both Catford and Croydon, and had included the handful of TTA2s, which were also withdrawn. A total of 76 TS3A type buses went to Croydon garage, these operating routes 12A, 54A, the 59 group, and the 75. Catford had 74 buses working on routes 36, 36A, 47, 47A, 54A and 75. Each garage had five extra buses to cover for breakdowns and regular overhaul of buses, and usually the same vehicles were retained as spares. Croydon had an additional six TS3As which worked as peak hour 'extras' on route 59. Commencing Sunday 5th November 1922, two of the Croydon extras operated on route 37 between Peckham and Isleworth, working off

No. 931 (XH 9300) was the first of the new TS3A buses to work from Croydon garage on the 75 route and it continued to operate on this service for many years. It is seen here in Croydon on the way to Woolwich Free Ferry late in 1922.

the 59 route at Brixton. From the same date two extra buses of the TS3A type were operated on route 25 from Catford garage; these ran to Victoria on the 36 road then on the 25 to Seven Kings. At first these ran daily but from 26th November they ran on Sundays only. The buses on the 25 ceased on 11th February and those on the 37 on 25th March 1923. The reason for these special workings is believed to be that Tilling's longer wheelbase buses were tried out on the difficult acute turn from Oxford Street to Bond Street on route 25. The experiment, if such it was, must have been successful as the LGOC replaced the K type on the route with the larger S type buses on 12th March 1923. There may have been some troublesome spot on the 37 route as larger buses did not work on the route until after the Tilling trials had ceased.

Tilling continued the practice started in 1904 of numbering all their motor fleet, whether buses, vans, or lorries, in one continuous series. The largest proportion of these numbers continued to be allocated to the sizeable contract fleet operated. The TTA1s had first been numbered intermittently between 140 and 249 with the final batch 300 to 406. By 1921, fleet numbers had reached 800 and the first TS3A for London was 805 followed by 813, then 815 to 899, the last ones to make up the total of 166 running from 916 to 994. In the meantime, TS3s and TS3As had been delivered to the Brighton fleet and by August 1922 seventy were in service in the town with somewhat different bodies, but with the same colour scheme as that used in London and also the same style of fleetname. Their numbers were also intermingled with the lorry and van fleet between 531 and 798 and between 906 to 915 followed by 1002. Brighton then ordered 33 more TS3As for developing their routes a year or two later, and these took the fleet numbers up to 1175.

The original position for the fleet number on Tilling's motors was on the chassis frame behind the back wheel, but when bus numbered 916 entered service it had been moved forward and was now situated on the chassis frame below the driver's cab, and the earlier buses soon followed suit. In the TTA1 days the registration number in the front had been at first placed in front of the bonnet on the nearside, but from 1916 onwards this was changed to a position below the service number in the centre of the driver's canopy, and this became standard for all Tilling motor buses both in the London and the Brighton fleets.

Another important event in 1922 occurred on 5th August when a chocolate liveried Leyland bus with the fleetname 'Express' entered service. This marked the start of the independents' challenge to the established companies and it caused the LGOC and the smaller companies like Tilling to look to their laurels in the face of direct competition. A bigger blow came to Tilling on 12th November 1922, when Percy Frost Smith, formerly

Tilling's chief engineer and one of the chief designers of the petrol-electric, began working between Lee Green and Liverpool Street with a revised form of petrol-electric bus assembled to his own design by Dennis Bros.

One of the last route changes in 1922 occurred on 6th December when the 59 (Camden Town and Thornton Heath) was withdrawn and its six buses added to the 15 on the 59B route (Camden Town and Coulsdon), which was then renumbered 59. It then had a total of 21 buses, and nine 'S' type Generals from Streatham (AK) completed the total of 30 needed to provide a frequency of 7½ minutes. Commencing 27th December, the 54 and 54A routes terminated at Strand (Aldwych) instead of Charing Cross. One Tilling bus was taken off the 54A and put on to the 59, thereby releasing one of the Streatham Generals, indicating the way that Tilling buses were kept in service as much as possible.

The 54 and 54A routes were again changed on 28th February 1923 when they were extended from the Strand to West Kilburn via Edgware Road and Shirland Road. The journey time for the 54A was increased to 126 minutes, which was considered too much for the Croydon-based buses, which were taken off and replaced General buses on the 59, the Tilling total becoming 31. The 54A allocation became eight General 'K' type from Nunhead garage, together with 11 Tillings from Catford, the five remaining on the 36A being used to make up the total. The 36A then had General buses only.

Summer Sunday operation had by now taken on considerable significance in London and involved a different route network to that of weekdays. Details of this operation with regard to Tilling will be studied in a later chapter, but certain high summer services affected also the regular workings of established Tilling's routes. During the winter months, the 47s had been worked exclusively by Tilling, 15 buses on the 47 and 12 on 47A. From 16th May, the full service operated through to Farnborough with an increased frequency and it now needed 43 buses, the LGOC supplying 24 K type buses from Dalston. The 12 TS3As from the 47A were divided between three routes, four to the 47, making a total of 19 buses, and five to the 36, increasing its headway to six minutes. The other three went on to the 75, and these replaced a similar number from Croydon garage where the extra buses were wanted for the 59 and 59A. The revised schedule provided for a ten-minute service to Coulsdon and a 30-minute one to Reigate with 25 buses, and the 59A was increased to every ten minutes to Caterham with 26 Tilling buses.

This was the last change in Tilling bus workings before a further agreement with the LGOC made it possible for a considerable increase in Tilling's London operations to come into force, and this will be covered in the next chapter. The weekday disposition of buses and routes is summarised below.

SUMMARY FOR MAY 16th 1923

Route	Detail	Garage	Buses	Joint
12A	Oxford Circus – South Croydon 'Red Deer'	Croydon	10	with AH
36	West Kilburn – Hither Green Station	Catford	33	—
47	Shoreditch Church – Farnborough	Catford	19	with D
54A	West Kilburn – South Croydon 'Swan and Sugar Loaf'	Catford	11	with AH
59	Camden Town – Reigate	Croydon	25	—
59A	Camden Town – Caterham	Croydon	26	—
75	Woolwich Free Ferry – South Croydon 'Red Deer'	Croydon	15	—
		Catford	11	—

5 More Joint Working and Co-operation 1923-1929

XH 9272, a 59A bus on its way to Caterham, is seen in St James Road, Croydon on 5th August 1923 on a temporary diversion due to tramway reconstruction in the main London Road.

On 10th April 1923, a supplementary agreement was made between the LGOC and Tilling which provided for the LGOC to acquire 166 Tilling-Stevens petrol-electric buses to be licensed in the name of Tilling and worked by them jointly with General's own buses. The number of buses to be worked at any one time was not limited, and it was arranged that the joint fleet should receive its share of the London Omnibus Pool on the basis of mileage worked. Tilling was to retain 50% in respect of its own buses, and out of the balance of 50% to deduct working expenses in respect of LGOC-owned buses. Out of this 50% it would also pay to the LGOC agreed sums for interest on capital and for depreciation, and divide the net profit subsequently arrived at in the proportion 70% to LGOC and 30% to Tilling. It was further provided that in the event of the total fleet in the London Omnibus Pool exceeding 3,320, Tilling should be entitled to provide 5% of the total. The 166 LGOC buses licensed in Tilling's name thus provided a fleet available for transfer to Tilling ownership from time to time with only accountancy adjustments and no licensing variations. These 166 buses went into service between July 1923 and December 1924.

A subsequent agreement between the two parties was made on 20th October 1925 in respect of Tilling's working 12 single-deck buses for a special route, and there was a further agreement on 6th August 1926 regarding Timpson's buses, whose 20 vehicles were bought by the LGOC early in 1926 and re-sold to Tilling, who began operating them on 25th March of that year. A modification was made under a new agreement dated 11th July 1929 which replaced all previous ones, and provided that as from 1st July, Tilling should be entitled to own and work on its own 5% of the buses in the London Pool, its total on that date being 240. The original Tilling figure of 166 had previously been increased by 20 buses from Timpson and by the transfer to Tilling ownership on that day of 54 of the LGOC petrol-electrics (for £28,000) which were in Tilling livery. The balance worked by Tilling for LGOC then became 124 (166 less 54 plus 12 single deckers). They continued to be worked as a joint fleet, and it was arranged that they should operate as far as possible the average daily mileage of all other buses in the London Pool. A subsequent adjustment in the 5% basis brought Tilling's own fleet up to 250 and reduced the fleet worked for LGOC to 114.

The effect of the 1923 agreement was to double the size of Tilling's working fleet to 300 buses and in order to house the additional vehicles the LGOC proposed to build two new garages, one at Bromley and one at Sidcup. In the event, Tilling did not wish to accept the Sidcup garage, so as an alternative Catford garage was considerably enlarged, and together with Bromley provided the necessary extra space. The new buses were Tilling-Stevens TS7 type, specially designed and incorporating modifications to meet the strict dictates laid down by Scotland Yard for London operation. The wheelbase was 14ft 9in and this type was restricted to this one order. They were to the forward-control style (driver beside engine) as opposed to the normal control of the TS3A type, and this was the main outward difference between the two classes worked by Tilling. A similar 48-seat body was built by Tilling at their own body works. The TS3As had been numbered in Tilling's own series between 805 and 994, but these new buses were put into a new series and numbered O 1 to O 166. The fleet number was shown on each side of the bus at the front of the chassis frame. The O and the number

were closed up on the vehicles, so that the O could equally have been read as a nought.

The gradual introduction of these new buses in 1923 and 1924 forms an interesting chapter in the Tilling story, with the vehicles being used to strengthen existing services and to take over additional routes from LGOC. The present account will concern itself with weekday operation, a subsequent chapter being devoted to the many and varied Sunday duties.

Registration numbers to coincide with the fleet numbers were obtained for the new buses, viz XN 7301-7350 for O 1-50, XP 2351-2400 for O 51-100, XR 701-750 for O 101-150. As always, Tilling were most methodical in introducing these new buses, licensing them in strict rotation and allocating them in order to specific routes and duties, many staying on such duties for several years. Certain buses were earmarked as spares to cover for breakdowns and overhauls, and at first this was every eleventh bus, namely O 11, O 22, O 33, and O 44, and later O 50, all being allocated to Catford garage. By December 1923, a total of 74 TS7s had been delivered and most were used in replacement of General buses.

Left and Below Right **Two views of O 1, a new bus designed and built in the summer of 1923. This was the first of 166 buses bought by the LGOC but built and operated by Tilling. A similar 48-seat body to that on the TS3A type is mounted on the forward control TS7 chassis.**

Bottom Right **Interior of the lower deck of O 1, giving an idea of the standard Tilling body of the time.**

The first routes chosen for the joint operation were 21 (Wood Green and Sidcup), 21A (Wood Green and Shooters Hill) and 21B (Wood Green and Farningham), which General operated with 'S' type buses from Palmers Green garage in the north and Old Kent Road in the south. It was the latter's vehicles that were replaced by the new Tilling buses. The first five, O 1-5, entered service on route 21A on Wednesday 25th July 1923 from Catford garage, followed by O 6-10 a week later. The next five buses, O 12-16, went on to the long 21B route on 29th August and on 5th September O 17-21 started work on the 21 service.

On 3rd October six new buses, O 23-28, were put on to route 36 in order to release six TS3A type for transfer to Croydon garage required as 'extras' on route 59. This transfer was further complicated for some reason as the six older buses from the 36 went on to route 47 and it was six from that service that went to Croydon. The next four new buses, O 29-32, went on to the 21A on 10th October, and with the introduction of the winter schedules on 17th October, O 34-38 joined route 21. The 47 lost four of its TS3A buses at the same time and two went on to route 54A, bringing the total up to 13. The other two were put on to route 36, releasing two of the new TS7s which were added to route 21 to make up its total of new buses. However, in 24th October, five more new buses, O 39-43, started work on the 21 as extras.

Turning to Croydon, the winter schedules saw an increased frequency on route 12A, which now acquired a six-minute headway, and whilst LGOC supplied more buses from Nunhead, Tilling increased their allocation to 19 with nine buses from the 59A. There was a strike at Croydon garage on 21st October as the men did not approve of the new 'spread-over' shifts in the new winter schedules. All the crews returned to work on Tuesday 23rd October.

The new buses in November started to work route 47, replacing part of LGOC's allocation from Dalston. These commenced on 7th November with O 45-49, followed by another five, O 51-55, on 21st November. Thus the 47 was made up of 15 TS3As and ten new TS7s, but this was altered in December as new buses continued to enter service on the 47 whilst displaced vehicles operated other routes. First, there was a return of Tilling to the 36A (West Kilburn and Grove Park) and six duties were allocated from 5th December using five TS3As from route 47 together with one spare. In their place, O 56-60 entered service on the 47. A week later on 12th December, Tilling buses replaced General's on route 1, the route being altered at the same time to run from Willesden rather than Cricklewood to Lewisham. Five TS3As from the 47 took over duties from Old Kent Road and O 61-65 replaced them on the 47. Finally on 19th December, the last TS3As from the 47 were put on to route 1, making a total of ten, and O 66-70 brought the total of new buses on the 47 to 25. As 1923 closed, Catford were operating 133 Tilling buses, 68 TS3As and 65 of the new TS7s, with a further five TS7s as spares or training vehicles, and four new vehicles which had just been delivered but not yet allocated.

On 2nd January 1924, O 71-74 entered service on the 36 route and then on 16th January a new weekday route 66 was introduced between Bostall Woods and Bromley Common to combat the troublesome competition with Messrs Timpson's service over these roads. LGOC provided 12 buses from Plumstead garage and Tilling introduced six new TS7s, O 75-80. LGOC had been

O 57 is seen on the Tilling-Stevens stand at the Commercial Motor Show at Olympia before entering service on route 47 in 1923. The board indicating 'Cheap 1d and 2d mid-day fares' had to be displayed during the times such reduced fares were in force.

A scene in Lee High Road, showing O 40 on route 21A bound for Wood Green and two LCC trams on route 46 operating to and from Woolwich.

operating this as a Sunday only service between Bostall Woods and Green Street Green since July 1923 with 17 buses from Plumstead garage. This continued with the addition of the six new Tillings. A route change on 16th January saw services 21 and 21B curtailed at Newington Green but 21A continued to Wood Green.

Beginning on 13th February the 54 and 54A routes were again revised. The 54 (West Kilburn and Keston) was withdrawn and the 54A was renumbered 54 and curtailed to operate between Oxford Circus and South Croydon with the frequency increased to ten minutes. General supplied 11 buses from Old Kent Road and Tilling continued with its 13 TS3As. Additional LGOC and Tilling buses were put on to the 66 from 12th March, the new TS7s being O 81-87.

The opening of Bromley garage (coded TB) coincided with the introduction of the summer schedules on 16th April, and it was the time for an amount of reorganisation. The initial allocation consisted of 54 new TS7s; 18 transferred from Catford (O 70-87) and 36 brand new ones (O 88-123). Bromley took over the operation of two routes from Catford, the 47 (Shoreditch and Farnborough) and the 66 (Plumstead Common and Bromley Common) which was extended to Green Street Green daily. An increased service was provided on the 47 using 42 buses, 35 from Bromley and seven Generals from Dalston. The Bromley allocation on the 66 was 16 buses. In true Tilling fashion, the 47s were numbered in order, O 71 being TB1 followed by the 66 from O 107, and three were spares.

At the same time a number of Catford routes were revised as the 25 buses removed from the 47 were redistributed and the 36A and 21B were taken over entirely by LGOC once more. The six TS3As from the 36A together with five TS7s from the 47 were put onto route 1 bringing its total to 21. Two routes new to Tilling now received an allocation from Catford, these being the 12B which worked from East Acton to Lower Sydenham (Bell Green) joint with General, and the 136 operating between Lewisham, Keston and Westerham Hill. These two routes needed nine TS7s each.

On 7th May 1924, Tilling took over operation of route 109 (Penge Tram Terminus and Chislehurst) for the LGOC, working it from Bromley garage, as General then did not have a garage conveniently situated for the route. Single deckers had to be used as the route was plagued by a number of low railway bridges, and 12 LGOC B type 26-seat buses were handed over to Tilling to work under an agreement similar to that which had applied to route 71 from Croydon between April and October 1922.

On Saturday 26th April 1924, the British Empire Exhibition at Wembley was opened by HM King George V and to cater for visitors to the exhibition the LGOC put on a number of special bus services from various parts of the London area. It had one of the first bus stations, with eight separate platforms. Among these special routes was the 36A (Grove Park and West Kilburn) which was diverted at Edgware Road and extended to Wembley by way of Cricklewood and the North Circular Road. It was operated by the LGOC with 22 of the new NS type buses from Old Kent Road garage, but from 7th May Tilling was able to join in the Wembley operation by putting five TS7 type buses on to the 36A, replacing a similar number of Generals. Five new buses were sent to Bromley garage and put on the 66 route and, by redistribution, five earlier buses, O 71-75, were transferred to Catford for use on the 36A. This procedure was repeated on 21st May and again on the 4th June so that older buses O 76-79 and 81-86 were passed to Catford for working on the 36A, making its allocation 15 TS7s and seven Generals. O 80 passed to Catford for use as a spare.

Interior of Bromley garage taken about a month after it opened in 1924 showing some of the new TS7 buses allocated for routes 47 and 136. A General single-deck B type for the 109 route is seen at the back.

Many special bus routes were put on for the British Empire Exhibition at Wembley in 1924. A General bus, NS 642, is seen at platform 1 of the bus station whilst on the 36A route from Grove Park, working from Old Kent Road garage. Tilling took over this service with TS7 buses later in the year.

In May 1924 Tilling took over the operation of single-deck route 109 from the LGOC together with twelve B type buses transferred from Nunhead garage, which had been working the route from some distance away. The new Bromley garage was on the line of route. B 5067, one of the buses for the service, is seen standing outside Nunhead garage. The rabbit mascot was carried by buses running on country routes.

The 1924 Derby at Epsom was held on 4th June and many LGOC and Tilling buses used for taking people to the famous horse race and retained as grandstands sank into the mud on the parking ground on what proved to be a very wet day, spending two days in the open before being retrieved. One week later, on Wednesday 11th June, a considerable reallocation of Tilling buses took place. This came about partly by the opening of the new LGOC bus garage at Sidcup, coded SP, when General S type buses took over routes 21 and 21B. Route 66 was withdrawn and so additional buses were placed on to route 47, the Bromley allocation being increased to 43 as part of the service was extended to Green Street Green, an extension previously undertaken by the 66. Route 136 was transferred from Catford to Bromley garage and worked by nine buses, though Catford did place extra buses on this route on Sundays. Service 54 was withdrawn between Oxford Circus and Lewisham and diverted to Plumstead Common in partial replacement for the 66. Tilling buses were taken off the 54 on account of the Southern Railway Company's ruling that only the B and K General buses with their lighter weight could be allowed over Ashburton Bridge in the Addiscombe Road. Forty Tilling buses from Catford were therefore available for redistribution. Three more went on to the 21A, making a total of 21, twelve TS7s went on to the 36 to replace Generals introduced in April when the frequency was increased to every four minutes, and seven TS7s were put on to 36A, making this service to Wembley entirely Tilling. The other 18 buses enabled Tilling to take over the major part of route 78 (Shoreditch and Dulwich) which had been worked by General since 1919. The LGOC continued to work eight K type from Camberwell garage to complete the quota for the route.

Tilling's 18 buses were made up by thirteen TS3As off the 54 and five TS7s. Hitherto, only the 36 and for a time the 47 had worked both types of Tilling vehicles. The 78 buses had long 'when working' or garage runs morning and night between Catford garage and Dulwich (Grove Hotel) by way of Stanstead Road and Forest Hill, already used by buses on the 12B and later by the 12A. One other change that day was the extension of route 1 on weekdays from Willesden to Wembley, providing Tilling's second service to the Exhibition.

On 25th June the next six new TS7 buses, although sent to Bromley garage, were put on to the 36 service, replacing six Generals and giving Tilling the full service of 51 buses. It meant another long garage journey from Bromley Common to Catford (St Laurence Church) to enter service. Nearly two months later, on 20th August, eight more TS7s were sent to Bromley for use on the 36. This released eight earlier O type at Catford, which were put on to route 12A in replacement of eight General S type, so once more extra journeys were needed from Catford garage to take up service at Forest Hill. These were the first Catford buses on the 12A and also the first TS7s. The duty numbers were changed, with the Catford buses being first as TL1 to TL8 and Croydon followed with TC9 to TC27. This had been the practice when services were operated by two garages; the 75 ran as TL1 to TL11 and TC12 to TC26, and the 54A commenced as TL1 to TL6 and TC7 to TC16.

On Thursday 11th September 1924 the last TS7 (O 166) was licensed and put into service at Bromley. The registrations of the last 16 TS7 type did not coincide with fleet numbers, being XT 8773 to XT 8788 (151-166). During the summer seven more TS7 buses, O 87-93, were transferred from Bromley to Catford garage all

54

Bromley's O 147 is the first of three buses standing outside the 'Falcon Hotel' at West Kilburn, the terminus of the 36 route for many years. The board has already been changed for the return journey to Hither Green Station.

being used as spares, but five spare TS3As were transferred from Catford to Croydon. Bromley garage still continued to operate these vehicles in strict rotation, rearranging them each time the earlier buses were sent to Catford. By the 11th September 1924 there were 73 buses at Bromley, O 94-166, seven of which were in use as spares, O 100, O 110, O 120, O 130, O 140, O 150, and O 160. The allocations, omitting the spares, were: 47, TB1 (O 94) to TB43 as O 141; 136, TB1 (O 142) to TB9 (O 151); 36, TB38 (O 152) to TB51 (O 166), Catford working up to TL37 at that time. On the same date, Catford had 161 buses made up of 68 TS3As and 93 TS7s, 14 being in use as spares. Croydon only had the TS3A type, totalling 98 including ten in use as spares. These spares at each garage were available for replacement of buses undergoing regular overhauls, for breakdowns and for Private Hire, which was most important during Wembley Exhibition years 1924/25.

The 1924 winter programme for London bus services of the LGOC and associated companies came into force on Monday 3rd November following the seasonal closure of the British Empire Exhibition the previous Saturday. The additional buses and the special routes to Wembley, as well as extra summer country services, were withdrawn. Another rearrangement of Tilling bus workings took place with the takeover of two more weekday routes. The revisions which provided the extra buses were as follows: the Bromley fleet was reduced by two buses, and O 94 and O 95 were transferred to Catford and used as spares, releasing two TS3As to Croydon. The winter service on the 47 needed only 32 buses, 28 from Bromley and four Generals from Dalston. Although the separate number 47A was no longer used, only 17 of these buses ran beyond Bromley Common

(Crown) to Farnborough. The 136 was also considerably reduced to a half-hour frequency between Keston and Lewisham, which only needed four buses. These reductions enabled another 17 buses to be put on the 36, for which duties were revised placing Bromley first (TB1 to TB31), Catford only supplying 19 as TL32 to TL50. Thus 18 Catford buses were available for reallocation, as well as another five from the reduction on the 36A which had been withdrawn from Wembley and diverted back to West Kilburn once more. Tilling were now able to take over part of the 12, the short workings between Oxford Circus and Dulwich (The Plough). The 18 buses provided a six-minute peak hour service reduced to 12 minutes at other times. This was another mixed allocation involving 12 TS7s and six TS3As. Three buses were put on as extras on the 36 on Mondays to Fridays and on the 21A on Saturdays. From 26th November they ran on the 21 on Mondays to Fridays also, when this service was revised. Three more Catford buses joined the eight on the 12A. This released three Croydon buses on that service which were needed for the other new Tilling working. This was part of route 34 (Liverpool Street and South Croydon), Tilling supplying 20 buses and LGOC another 22. The required number was obtained by a reduction of eleven buses on route 59A, four from 59, as well as the three from the 12A and the two ex-Catford buses.

On 26th November 1924, the 21 and 21A routes were revised. The seven-minute headway on each was replaced by four-and-a-half minutes on the 21 and nine minutes on 21A, with the result that the 24 Tilling buses were moved from the 21A to the 21, joining the 28 Generals from Sidcup, the LGOC covering the 21A from Palmers Green.

A traffic scene outside Liverpool Street Station showing a TS3A Tilling on the weekday working of route 34 sharing the terminus with LGOC buses on routes 7 and 11. The date is 1926 and a recently-introduced covered-top bus on the 11 can be seen on the stand.

Tilling undertook a considerable amount of private hire work in addition to bus operation, using both buses and coaches for this purpose. Here, a typical group of young people of the period pose alongside TS3A XH 9298.

Old Number	New Number	Detail
1	No change	Willesden and Lewisham
12	12c	Oxford Circus and Dulwich
12A	No change	Oxford Circus and South Croydon
12A(Sun)	12E	Shepherds Bush and S Croydon
12B	112	East Acton and Lower Sydenham
21	21A	Wood Green and Sidcup
21A	20	Wood Green and Shooters Hill
21B	21	Wood Green and Farningham
34	No change	Liverpool St and South Croydon
36	No change	West Kilburn and Hither Green
36A	136	West Kilburn and Grove Park
47	No change	Shoreditch and Green Street Green
47	47A	Shoreditch and Farnborough
47	47B	Shoreditch and Bromley Common
59	No change	Camden Town and Reigate
59A	59A	Camden Town and Coulsdon
59	59B	Camden Town and South Croydon
59A	159	Camden Town and Godstone
59A	159A	Camden Town and Caterham
75	No change	Woolwich and South Croydon
78	No change	Shoreditch and Dulwich
109	No change	Penge and Chislehurst
136	146	Lewisham and Westerham Hill
136	146A	Lewisham and Keston

The numbers of two of these routes were altered in April 1925 to provide for the summer extensions and possible projection to Wembley, route 1 being listed as Wembley to Sidcup and 136 as Wembley to Bromley Common. Although route 1 was not extended to Wembley for the second year it was renumbered as 1B, Willesden and Sidcup, and 1C, Willesden and Lewisham. The LGOC began on 8th April a route with single-deck buses between Lewisham and Bromley Common via Grove Park as 136D, so from that date the West Kilburn and Grove Park route became 136A. There was no extension to Wembley that year. The summer Sunday extension of the 78 to Bromley Common resulted in the Shoreditch and Dulwich route being renumbered 78A.

The first change in Tilling operation in 1925 occurred on Wednesday 18th February when the 12C was withdrawn and replaced by new route 120A from Dulwich (Plough) to Sudbury Town Station, supporting General route 120 between Dulwich and Harrow Weald. The 19 buses for the 120A were provided by 18 from the 12C plus one extra from the 136, where it was found possible to do the same work with one bus fewer. The 120A was not a success, and both it and 120 were withdrawn on 7th April and the 12C was reinstated the next day.

The summer programme for 1925 was introduced on 15th April. At Croydon, services 59 and 159A were revised and the Tilling buses redistributed with 21 for the 59 and 59A, and 19 for the 159A. In south-east London, the 47 was reinstated between Shoreditch and Green Street Green with a half-hourly frequency to the southern outpost during the week and every eight minutes on Sunday. The four buses that had been on the 146A were now added to the 47's total and LGOC took over total operation of both the 146 and 146A. When the winter schedules were introduced on 18th November, the 47's extension to Green Street Green continued at a reduced frequency, and similar reductions on the 59 route meant only an hourly operation to Reigate with five Croydon buses and 12 on the 59A. This was the yearly pattern of service established on routes 59 and 47 over the next few years.

The London Traffic Act 1924 came into force on 1st December that year and it required that all omnibus routes in the Metropolitan Police Area be registered with the Police, who were responsible for approving the terminal points, the route to be followed and the number of buses on each route. This was necessary due to the large number of buses put on to the roads since 1922 by Independent companies. The route numbers also came under the control of the Police and this resulted in a considerable amount of renumbering under what was known as the 'Bassom System' named after Superintendent Bassom of the Public Carriage Office, who was in charge of these alterations. It provided that all variations of route should have a separate number, and suffix letters were added to indicate any short workings of the main route. All Tilling routes were approved and were renumbered as follows:

Interior of Croydon garage in 1925 after the Bassom system of route numbering had come into force, showing a line-up of TS3A buses operating on routes 12A, 34, 75A and 159A. The side service number is shown by a white board on the top deck instead of by illuminated numbers in the centre of the lower deck windows, a change which took place on TS3A and TS7 buses when the Bassom system was introduced.

The 12C service had a mixed fleet of TS3A and TS7 type buses and O 48, one of the latter, is waiting on the stand outside the 'Plough' Dulwich whilst a General, K 819, on the longer 112B route stands further back.

A rear view of O 170, one of twelve single-deck TS7 type buses purchased by the LGOC to replace the B type on the 109 service. Although operated by Tilling from TB garage these buses were in standard General livery.

When taken over from LGOC in 1924, the 109 worked on a 12-minute frequency between Chislehurst and Penge Tram Terminus (Thicket Road). On 18th February 1925, the route was withdrawn between Thicket Road and 'Crooked Billet' and this shortened route was numbered 109A. Under a subsidiary agreement between Tilling and LGOC, the latter agreed to purchase 12 TS7 type single-deck buses for this service. The 30-seat bodies were constructed by Tilling, and when they commenced operation on 7th October, they were painted in standard LGOC livery with the GENERAL fleetname. Later, they were repainted into Tilling livery. They were numbered O 168-179; the number O 167 had been given to a TS7 lorry allocated to Bromley garage. Ten of these new buses provided a ten-minute frequency and O 170 and O 179 were spares.

TS3A No. 896 is standing at the 'Old Surrey Hounds', the terminus of the 159A route in Caterham, before it proceeds on the long journey to Camden Town in the summer of 1926. By this time all TS3A buses had been fitted with a driver's shield bearing the Tilling fleetname similar to those on the later TS7 class.

The most serious competition experienced by Tilling arose from A. Timpson & Son who introduced a fleet of silver painted Straker-Squire buses in 1923 on a route between Plumstead Common and Bromley. After purchase by LGOC the Company was sold in 1926 to Tilling and the buses operated from Bromley Garage. XR 3517 is seen at Plumstead after being overhauled by Tilling, the registration number being moved to the canopy over the driver and running numbers added.

The only serious competition experienced by Tilling in their territory during this time was from Alexander Timpson and Son who, in March 1923, introduced a fleet of silver-painted Straker-Squire buses which by April 1924 had reached 18 in number. After a few initial experiments, Timpson settled down to operate one route

between Plumstead Common and Bromley Common (Southlands Road) with extensions to Green Street Green and Westerham Hill. At first these routes were un-numbered but they came within the provisions of the London Traffic Act and so under the Bassom scheme they became:

213   Plumstead Common and Westerham Hill.
289   Plumstead Common and Green Street Green.
289A Plumstead Common and Bromley Common.

From July 1923, the LGOC had attempted to combat this competition by extending service 2A from Catford to Plumstead Common on weekdays, and introducing the 66 on Sundays between Plumstead Common and Green Street Green. Then in January 1924 the 66 was extended to Bostall Woods and introduced as a daily service worked jointly by LGOC and Tilling, with the 2A being cut back to Catford once more. Eventually, on 25th March 1926, LGOC was able to purchase the Timpson bus service and it was immediately resold to Tilling. Alexander Timpson Ltd continued to operate coaches, and so it was necessary to set up a new company, Timpson's Omnibus Services Ltd. The 20 buses were then operated by Tilling under this name from Bromley garage. Although the buses retained the silver livery and the Timpson fleetname, all of the Straker-Squires were overhauled by Tilling, and took on the 'Tilling Style' appearance. Registration numbers were placed in the standard Tilling position under the route number box, and TB plates and duty numbers were fitted.

The Timpson fleet had been increased by the acquisition of six blue Frost Smith buses, these petrol-electrics having been designed and operated by Percy Frost Smith, the former engineer of Thomas Tilling. His independent concern had attempted to operate these six buses on a long route between Hanwell and Bromley Common (or Farnborough), but it was not successful, and they were withdrawn just before Mr Frost Smith's death on 24th December 1924. Timpson had then added these buses to the fleet in March 1925, but only two had been retained as buses. Tilling found these two most unsatisfactory, and two much older Straker-Squire chassis which had previously been charabancs were acquired from Timpson, and the bus bodies from the two FS vehicles mounted.

In 1927 Tilling obtained from the LGOC five Tilling-Stevens buses which had been acquired from Cambrian Landray and had once been charabancs. Tilling added these to the Timpson fleet. Four of them had unusual Irish registrations and IT 302 is seen on its way to Bromley Common on the 289A route.

Another ex-Cambrian Landray vehicle which was passed to Tilling was XB 9888, a Tilling-Stevens charabanc. This was fitted with a double-deck bus body in February 1927 and became number 56 in the Timpson fleet. It is photographed at Plumstead Common in October 1927.

During 1927 Tilling added further Tilling-Stevens buses to the Timpson fleet by mounting the bodies off the Straker-Squires on to TS3 chassis that had previously been charabancs or lorries. XH 9758 is seen at Bromley Common, the Timpson fleet number 62 being shown on the chassis frame in Tilling fashion.

Early in 1927 the LGOC took over the business of an independent operator, Cambrian Landray, which had operated five Tilling-Stevens buses, originally charabancs but rebodied as double-deck buses. Four of these had Irish 'IT' registrations which looked most unusual. LGOC passed these five buses on to Tilling in exchange for five Straker-Squires, and the Tilling-Stevens painted in Timpson's silver livery entered service from Bromley garage during March 1927 on route 289A. Between April and October 1927, Tilling replaced the remaining 15 Straker-Squire buses by removing their bodies and fitting them to TS3 chassis which had been lorries or charabancs. The silver livery continued to be carried, but this changed on 1st January 1928 when Thomas Tilling Ltd absorbed the Timpson's Omnibus Services Ltd and all 20 buses were painted in the standard Tilling livery. The extension of the 289 to Green Street Green was adequately covered by the 47, and so Tilling operated 17 buses on route 289A on weekdays and, during the summer months, worked 19 buses on the 213 route on Sundays, reducing to just four in the winter months when 289A ran as well.

The Timpson fleet was repainted into Tilling livery in 1928, and this picture shows XM 2992, another ex-Cambrian Landray bus, on the summer Sunday route 213 on its way to Westerham Hill. The Tilling fleet number 1217 is seen on the chassis frame.

Below Two former Timpson buses are seen standing outside 'The Old Mill', the Plumstead Common terminus of the 289A route, in 1928.

Only a few of the many Independent buses that ran in London operated for any length of time on Tilling routes, but the one bus owned by Carswool, a Leyland LB new in 1924, ran for many years on route 21, even reaching Farningham as this picture shows. It retained its solid tyres up to 1933 when it passed to London Transport.

The Standard Omnibus Company had been operating a number of buses on the 12 route and in November 1929 obtained this Leyland TD1 (UW 6777), the first of four of that type. Although normally on the 112B from Shepherds Bush, it also ran on the 12C from Oxford Circus. It is seen in St Georges Road.

G.H. Allitt & Sons operated Leyland Titans on route 47A. This bus, GN 3185 new in January 1931, is seen outside the Gaumont Cinema in Lewisham.

Julius and Lockwood operated under the fleetname 'JL' and its Leyland LB new in 1926 is seen at the Hither Green terminus of the 36 in April 1928. The bus is on a short working to Victoria and had already been taken over by the London Public Omnibus Company, as the fleet number L35 shows.

During the General Strike of May 1926 a number of Tilling buses ran a special service under the number 12C between Dulwich and Oxford Circus manned by volunteer crews and with police protection. No. 834 (XF 9819) is seen in Peckham Road.

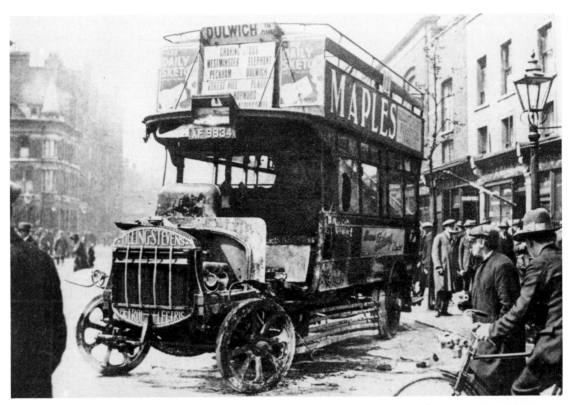

The uneasy industrial climate of the period culminated in the General Strike which started on 4th May 1926. All LGOC and Tilling crews withdrew their labour, although Tilling found that they could operate a limited service on route 12c between Dulwich and Oxford Circus from 6th May manned by members of the office staff and volunteers working from Bull Yard. Unfortunately, one bus (a TS3A, number 849) was attacked by incensed busmen and set alight in Walworth Road near the Elephant & Castle. Thereafter the route was changed to work via Kennington, and Walworth Road was avoided. As more volunteers became available additional buses were put on to the 12c and also other Tilling services. Only 3d and 6d fares were charged at first, but during the last two days of the strike normal fares applied. The General Strike was called off on 12th May.

Above **This bus, No. 849 (XF 9834), in service with a volunteer crew during the General Strike was attacked by striking busmen in Walworth Road and set alight. It was later towed back to Catford garage by a Tilling lorry.**

The windows of most of the buses operated during the General Strike had to be protected by netting. Following the incident in Walworth Road the 12C route was diverted via Kennington, as the notice on the side shows amidst other slogans including a message of support for prime minister Stanley Baldwin.

The period between 1925 and 1928 saw few changes to the Tilling routes. On 16th June 1926, single-deck route 109A was extended from Chislehurst to Eltham and renumbered 109. It used 11 Tilling buses from Bromley and three LGOC buses from Sidcup. Due to the extension of route 75 to Coulsdon on Sundays from 15th April 1927, the weekday service between Woolwich and South Croydon had to be renumbered 75F. The summer programme introduced from 25th May 1927 saw route 147 operating on weekdays as well as Sundays, with nine buses from Bromley garage. It was really an extension of the 47 from Green Street Green to Knockholt Pound, and had been introduced on Sundays the previous year.

A new type of bus radiator was introduced in December 1926 which read 'Thomas Tilling Ltd' on top of the tank and 'London & Brighton' on the bottom. Upon overhaul all the older style radiators were replaced.

Several of the routes working from Catford garage were still using a mixture of TS3As and TS7s, but early in 1927 it was found possible to change three of them when the 12 remaining TS3As on route 36 were replaced by eight TS7s from 12A and four from the 78. These latter two routes then became entirely TS3A. Since the opening of Bromley garage in 1924, the 47 route had been operated entirely by Tilling buses from that garage, apart from four Generals from Dalston. However, in August 1927 two buses were taken off the Bromley allocation of the 47 and put on to the 36, thereby releasing two Catford buses. These two together with one spare were put on to the 47, which enabled earlier morning and later night journeys to be operated between Catford and Bromley.

With the introduction of winter weekday schedules on 16th November 1927, Tilling obtained a dispensation from the Ministry of Transport enabling them to operate six additional buses on route 159A, replacing six Generals and being offset by three buses withdrawn for the winter months from route 59 and three from the 47.

All London buses had open-top decks until in 1925 the LGOC experimented with four NS type with covered tops. During the following years they gradually put more of this type into service, but Tilling did not experiment with covered-top buses until 1929. In the meantime LGOC put covered-top buses on to many of the routes they operated jointly with Tilling. For example, by June 1927 twenty covered-top NSs were on the 34 and on 7th September 1927 Dalston garage were working four on the 47. In October 1928 there were eight on the 78A from Camberwell garage and Nunhead ran 11 on the 12A.

Apart from seasonal changes with the 47 and 59 groups of routes, no major change had taken place with Tilling's routes in four years until 1929, when some revisions were necessary. Since 1925 concern had been expressed at the number of buses using some of the streets in the Metropolis, and under the London Traffic Act it was possible to reduce and regulate the numbers under Restricted Street Orders. These came later to the outer areas of London, and on 27th March 1929 the Croydon Restriction Order came into force limiting to some extent the bus services through the town. Coincidentally on the same day, LGOC opened their new garage at Elmers End which was given the code ED. Service 12A was revised and retimed, and General's 11 covered-top NSs now worked from Elmers End instead of Nunhead. One less Tilling bus was needed from both Catford and Croydon. Route 34 (Liverpool Street and South Croydon) was diverted between Norbury and West Croydon via Melfort Road and Thornton Heath and renumbered 133. This replaced the 58 which instead of using Melfort Road went straight down the London Road as did the 59, paralleling the latter route to Coulsdon and then on to Chipstead Valley Road at a reduced frequency. Route 159 was withdrawn between Norbury and Caterham or Godstone and diverted along Green Lane to terminate at Thornton Heath (Clock Tower). The 59 group was retimed, the 59 working to Reigate and the 59A to Coulsdon but with additional

O 82 is seen having just been overhauled and has been fitted with a new type of radiator introduced by Tilling in December 1926 which subsequently replaced the familiar Tilling-Stevens radiator on all petrol-electric vehicles in the fleet. This bus then returned to its duty as TL 11 on the 136A route.

Tilling's XH 9281 passes across Piccadilly Circus on its way to Reigate and is closely followed by K 17, a General bus on route 3B bound for Crystal Palace. Both buses are very full, an indication of travel during the evening peak.

peak hour buses between Camden Town and South Croydon as 59B. To replace the 159, route 75 was projected from South Croydon to Caterham Valley as 75D and through to Godstone on Sundays as the 75. Tilling buses were redistributed between the 59, 59A, 59B and 75, as General took over entirely the operation of the 133 and 159. Forty Croydon buses ran on the 59 and 59A with another 15 on 59B. The 75D was increased to 16 from Croydon and 17 from Catford. This allocation lasted only six weeks as on 15th May Croydon put three more buses on the 75D, releasing three from Catford's quota. These were needed for the 136A which from that date was extended from Grove Park to Bromley Common and renumbered 136, replacing single-deck 136D over this section.

The hinged flap on route boards was discontinued from 29th May 1929 as it was no longer a requirement by the Metropolitan Police who had previously insisted that the list of roads traversed should read in the direction of travel.

Wednesday 5th June 1929 saw a major revision to the 12 group of routes. Part of the 12C was extended from Oxford Circus to Mill Hill under the number 121. The 112B that General had been working between Dulwich and Shepherds Bush was extended to Park Royal as 112A, the off-peak journeys only working to Peckham Rye as 112C. The 112 (East Acton and Lower Sydenham) was renumbered 112E. At the Dulwich terminal, the buses were withdrawn from the 'Plough' stand, and sent on to 'Grove Hotel', already in use by the 78. The LGOC operated the 121, and also the new 82 service (East Acton and West Wickham) but the 12C and 112A were joint with Tilling, three peak hour buses working on 12C and 14 buses on 112A. A change from previous practice, by which each route's running numbers started at 1, took place and the Tilling duties on the 12 group were arranged in one sequence similar to that with LGOC on these routes, namely 12A, TL1-11, 12C, TL12-14, 112A, TL15-28, and 112E, TL29-36. In view of this the Croydon buses on 12A became TC1-15.

A number of Tilling buses from all three garages were in use in August and September 1929 for a major private hire job in transporting a large party of Scouts from Hungary on a visit to London. Buses are shown lined up outside Westminster Abbey.

By 1928 most bus operators were considering the replacement of the open-top buses by more modern covered-top vehicles but for a time this was not possible. The LGOC had nearly two years' experience with the covered-top NS class but these had their limitations as they were underpowered and it was not possible to fit them with pneumatic tyres until the Metropolitan Police had increased the permitted width on London buses in June 1928. The outlook changed with the advent of the Leyland Titan in 1928 and the AEC Regent in 1929 with low-slung chassis and six-cylinder engines.

Early in 1929 Thomas Tilling had under construction at the Pelican Yard works a 52-seat open staircase body with covered top deck. It was rather narrow, with a straight front to the top deck. Still loyal to the petrol-electric tradition, in February 1929 the Company obtained from Tilling-Stevens at Maidstone a TS17A chassis which was built of light alloy to keep down weight and fitted with 4-wheel brakes and pneumatic tyres. The covered-top body was mounted on this petrol-electric chassis and licensed on 30th April 1929, registered as GU 7750. It went into service on Saturday 18th May 1929 on route 36 running as TB30 from Bromley garage. A little over two months later, Tilling obtained from AEC a Regent demonstrator which had a 51-seat Short Brothers body and was registered UU 9161. This bus also joined the TS17A on route 36 from 28th July, with duty number TB14. This AEC bus eventually ran in Brighton from 10th to 30th December 1929. Tilling do not appear to have been completely satisfied with the original covered-top body, so during the summer another one was designed and built at Pelican Yard. This body was a great improvement and more to the style of the covered-top body eventually adopted; it was mounted on another TS17A chassis, registered GU 6483. It joined the other buses on route 36 on 11th October 1929.

The first covered-top bus operated by Tilling was GU 7750, a Tilling-Stevens TS17A which ran experimentally on route 36 from 18th May 1929. It had a rather narrow body with straight front to the top deck unlike later Tilling bus bodies.

View of GU 6483, the second TS17A bus to enter service in London on route 36, doing so in October 1929. It had a much improved style of body, being a prototype for bodies for Tilling's fleet of AEC Regents. The TS17A chassis were returned to the makers in 1930 and the bodies mounted on to AEC chassis for use in Brighton.

Left **An official photograph of the AEC Regent loaned to Tilling for trial purposes in July 1929 which, proving satisfactory, led to the Company abandoning petrol-electric transmission and ordering petrol engined buses. Right UU 9161 was operated on the 36 route and was fitted with standard route boards and service numbers taken from a TS7 bus.**

Thomas Tilling obtained one more TS17A chassis, which was mounted with an open-top body, registered as UU 9805 and used in Brighton from 31st October to 9th December 1929. They then decided that the covered-top petrol-electrics were unsuitable in service and all TS17A chassis were returned to the makers in April 1930, the three bodies being retained by Tilling and

mounted on some of the new AEC Regents delivered in 1930 and used in Brighton. How the company changed to the AEC Regent type of bus, which entered service in London in 1930, is told in a later chapter.

The following chart summarises the weekday allocation of scheduled buses at the high summer period for 1929.

WEEKDAY SCHEDULES FOR 3rd JULY 1929

Route	Details		Garage	Type	Number
1C	Willesden – Lewisham		TL	PE	21
12A	Oxford Circus – South Croydon		TL	PE	11
			TC	PE	15
			ED	*NS	11
12C	Oxford Circus – Dulwich		TL	PE	3
			ED	*NS	6
112A	Park Royal – Dulwich		AH	K	8
112C	Park Royal – Peckham Rye		TL	PE	14
			S	K	12
112E	East Acton – Lower Sydenham		TL	PE	9
			AH	K	6
			S	K	6
21A	Wood Green – Sidcup		TL	PE	24
			SP	S	19
36	West Kilburn – Hither Green		TB	PE	33
			TL	PE	15
136	West Kilburn – Bromley Common		TL	PE	20
47	Shoreditch – Green Street Green		D	*NS	4
147	Shoreditch – Knockholt Pound		TB	PE	28
			TL	PE	5
59	Camden Town – Reigate		TC	PE	40
59A	Camden Town – Coulsdon				
59B	Camden Town – South Croydon		TC	PE	15
			P	K	16
75D	Caterham – Woolwich		TL	PE	14
			TC	PE	19
78A	Shoreditch – Dulwich		TL	PE	18
			Q	*NS	8
109	Penge – Eltham		TB	†PE	11
			SP	†K	3
289A	Plumstead Common – Bromley Common		TB	PE	17

*Covered top   †Single-deck

6 Sunday and Bank Holiday Services 1921-1929

It was only on summer Sundays that route 1 operated to its full extent of Willesden to Chislehurst and 892 is passing through the Elephant and Castle on its way to the country in September 1930.

Certain bus services were not needed on Sundays or did not require as many vehicles; therefore the surplus buses could be used to advantage on special or extended routes at the weekend, particularly in the summer months.

The LGOC had operated nine special Sunday services in 1910 to places such as Hampton Court and Epping Forest. More extensive Sunday services were put on during the following years, thanks to the increasing numbers of the useful B type bus, and in the summer of 1914 over 30 special Sunday routes were operated that spread out much farther afield to such places as Hatfield and Epping Town in the north or to Dorking and Reigate in the south. After the First World War a regular annual programme of summer Sunday and bank holiday services was introduced commencing each year at Easter by starting on Good Friday. During May, a High Summer programme with additional routes and increased frequencies was put on. These summer services continued until late October or early November. Tilling's services were included in these annual programmes of special summer workings. Certain bus routes were changed on winter Sundays and reduced

services left many General buses idle, but Tilling managed to operate a full quota of buses all the year round. The various agreements with LGOC restricting the numbers of buses operated in London was not enforced on Sundays and the specific licensing of individual routes under the 1924 Road Traffic Act did not apply, hence the variety of routes that could be operated on this day.

Mention has been made of Sunday workings by Tilling prior to 1914. No significant change appears to have been made between weekday and Sunday operation during the war years or immediately afterwards. As far as Croydon garage was concerned some reallocation took place, mainly in the summer months, so that additional buses could be operated to Reigate, Caterham or Godstone. In October 1921, the 59 route was revised to work between Camden Town and Thornton Heath and this ran on weekdays only, so on Sunday 23rd October 11 TTA1 Tillings were put on to route 43 (Muswell Hill and South Croydon) worked jointly with six General buses. On weekdays the 43 terminated at London Bridge Station but since 1919 had on Sundays been extended to the Croydon area covering weekday route 34 (Liverpool Street and South Croydon). In December 1921 the 43 was extended in the north from Muswell Hill to Colney Hatch Lane. For the summer season, starting on Good Friday 14th April 1922, the 43 on Sundays was extended from South Croydon to Caterham with 17 Generals and only six Tillings, which by then were TS3A type. Tilling last ran on the 43 on Sunday 8th October 1922 and although the route continued to operate to the Croydon area until 1933, being extended to Caterham each summer, it was entirely General operated.

With effect from 30th March 1923, route 12A was on Sundays and bank holidays extended from Oxford Circus to Shepherds Bush, but this was too long a route for Croydon-based buses to work and so only LGOC vehicles were used. The ten buses off the 12A were on Sundays put on to route 19A (Highbury Barn and Thornton Heath), another joint working with General, working from Battersea garage (B). From October 1923 additional buses were available for Sunday work following the increased weekday allocation for the 12A to 19 buses. Starting Sunday 21st October, the 19A was diverted via Melfort Road instead of the main road to Thornton Heath and extended via Whitehorse Road to South Croydon, requiring 14 Tillings and two Battersea Generals. Tilling last ran on the 19A on Sunday 13th April 1924.

Another Sunday variation had started on 30th March 1923, when route 54A was operated between Lewisham and Riddlesdown, the buses actually terminating at the 'Whyteleafe Hotel'. This route was entirely worked by Tilling using 11 TS3As from Croydon and one from Catford garage. From 21st October 1923, this changed to six buses each from Catford and Croydon. The route was renumbered 54 from 20th February 1924 and withdrawn on 8th June the same year.

From 3rd November 1924, Tilling joined in the operation of the weekday only 34 service (Liverpool Street and South Croydon) and so its 20 buses and the 17 off the 12A were available for redistribution on Sundays. It was these 37 vehicles which enabled Croydon buses on routes 59 and 59A or 75 to be reallocated seasonally as required. However, Croydon had acquired another working, on which, although a daily route, Tilling took a share only on Sundays. Using as many buses as they had available, the numbers varied considerably during the following years. The route was the 49 (Shepherds Bush and Crystal Palace), a summer Sunday extension from Streatham Common. Tilling put 13 buses on the service from 15th June 1924, working from Croydon garage to Streatham Common to take up duty. Renumbering under the Bassom scheme on 1st December 1924 gave:

49 Shepherds Bush and Lewisham
49A Shepherds Bush and Streatham Common
49B Shepherds Bush and Crystal Palace (summer Sundays)

In view of a probable projection to Wembley, the Shepherds Bush and Lewisham service was renumbered 49C in April 1925. For the summer season, starting 10th April 1925, Tilling ran the 49B exclusively with 16 buses, and when the 49B was withdrawn for the winter on 8th November Tilling changed to the 49C with 24 buses, LGOC supplying another seven. The next summer, Tilling only managed 11 buses for 49B and so shared it with General, but from 17th October 1926 Tilling were able to operate the full 49C service with 31 buses. The

summer programme for 1927 saw all 92 Croydon buses needed for the 59, 159, and 75 services, so 49B and 49C were left entirely to the LGOC. The extra summer duties being withdrawn at the end of the season, from 23rd October 1927 Tilling returned to 49C with 25 buses, LGOC providing another five. Summer 1928 saw the two routes return entirely into the hands of the General, but on 21st October Tilling again found it possible to cover the entire 49C with 30 buses.

The drastic revision to services in the Croydon area on 27th March 1929 meant a complete reallocation of buses on Sunday as well from 31st March. The 49C now became a joint working, Croydon supplying 18 TS3As and Streatham 17 NSs. A new Sunday working for Tilling was the 58 (Camden Town to Chipstead Valley Road) using 15 buses. Route 75 had taken over the Caterham road from 159 and so on Sundays was extended to Godstone using 20 buses from Croydon and 16 from Catford. When the summer was over, additional buses were released so that Tilling could take over the whole of the 49C with 35 buses.

Until 1924, Catford garage did not see such a marked pattern of Sunday service variation except, of course, in the service on the 47 beyond Bromley Common. However with the coming of the O type and the opening of Bromley garage, several seasonal changes took place subsequently. Bromley had taken over routes 47 and 66, and from 20th April 1924 the latter was extended each end on Sundays to work between Bostall Woods and Green Street Green, although with no increase in the Tilling operation. Three Catford routes were developed for the summer months. Route 1 was extended from Lewisham to Sidcup, and twenty-one TS7s were put on the 21B (Wood Green and Farningham) at the expense of the 21 and 21A. The Lewisham, Keston and Westerham Hill route 136 received 11 Catford buses in addition to the nine from Bromley garage. As usual, the 47 maintained its summer Sunday extension to Green Street Green.

When Sidcup garage was opened in June 1924, route 21B was taken over entirely by LGOC, and so from 15th June Tilling put 19 buses on the 78A (Shoreditch and Bromley Common) which was in addition to ten buses working the 78 to Dulwich. From this time Catford was operating an average of 147 to 150 buses each Sunday.

The winter programme which came into force on 3rd November 1924, after the placing into service of the last TS7, initiated a greater difference between the weekday and Sunday services. This was due to some extent to the 18 buses operating on route 12 (later 12C) between Oxford Circus and Dulwich, which ran on weekdays only, and also to 19 buses from the 36 being surplus, as this service was left solely to Bromley on Sundays. Although Croydon buses were unable to work on the 12A on Sundays when extended to Shepherds Bush, it was possible for Tilling buses from Catford to join in this operation and in fact the eight TS7s put on to the route in August 1924 had worked on Sundays. So from 9th November 1924, Catford with 39 buses took over the major part of the Sunday 12A, which was renumbered 12E from 1st December. Another new Sunday working for Tilling from that date was the 53A (South Hampstead 'Swiss Cottage' and Abbey Wood) with 21 buses. This was renumbered 153 from 1st December.

Route 1 was again extended to Sidcup with 26 buses from Good Friday 10th April 1925, being renumbered as 1B. Also from that date the summer working between

Shoreditch and Bromley Common came back, this time as 78, the daily route to Dulwich becoming 78A. Tilling, put 12 buses on the 78 and the LGOC ran the 78A. This Bromley Common extension ceased at the end of that summer season and did not appear in subsequent years. Sixteen buses were put on to the 20 (Wood Green and Shooters Hill) instead of the 21A, but they were back on 21A in November with six additional buses. Although the 12C was only a weekday operation, between November 1925 and April 1926 eight Catford buses maintained a reduced service between Oxford Circus and Dulwich (Plough), the only time this ever occurred.

A variation of the 75 was tried from Good Friday 2nd April 1926 when it was withdrawn between Woolwich Ferry and Beresford Square and diverted to Plumstead Common (Woodman). It was renumbered 175 and the Catford allocation increased to 25 buses, whilst Croydon provided 12. This Sunday route met with little success, being withdrawn on 23rd May and the 75 reinstated. Sunday services on the 21 group were revised with Tilling working nine buses on the 20, five on the 21, and ten on 21A, all of these being joint with the General, who ran the major part of these routes. Sunday services were again revised from 20th June 1926, and Tilling gave up its operation on route 153. Fourteen of these buses were put on the 1B, which was extended to Chislehurst instead of Sidcup as in previous summers. The other seven buses were put on route 132 (Lewisham and Dartford, Westgate Road) replacing LGOC vehicles. This ceased in October, the 1C operating daily between Willesden and Lewisham.

From 23rd May 1926, sixteen Bromley buses started a new Sunday service 147 between Shoreditch and Knockholt Pound. It was provided by alternate buses on

the 47 continuing on beyond Green Street Green, which thus had an eight-minute headway, 16 minutes to Knockholt. From the same date the former Timpson service 289A was replaced on Sundays by route 213, which ran every 12 minutes between Plumstead Common and Westerham Hill with 19 buses. The 213 service continued on Sundays during the winter months at a 60-minute headway, being supplemented by additional buses each summer to a 30- or 15-minute frequency. This continued until 1930.

During the summers of 1927 and 1928, twenty buses were put on the 20 to Shooters Hill and 28 on the 21 to Farningham. Summer 1927 saw the LGOC operating the 78A on Sundays and Tilling covering the extension of the 1B to Chislehurst, whilst the following year, Tilling returned to the 78A and LGOC operated the 1B. In the winter of 1927 and throughout 1928, LGOC left the 12E route to Tilling, who used 47 buses to cover the entire service. Since 1925 the 146 route between Lewisham, Keston and Westerham Hill had been left to the LGOC, but on Sunday 26th August 1928, Tilling came back on to the route with three buses from Bromley. These were withdrawn in October but came back again from Sunday 27th March 1929, albeit for less than two months.

The LGOC buses returned to the 12E on 31st March 1929 following the opening of Elmers End garage, when the allocation was split with 17 buses from the new garage and 27 from Catford. This enabled Tilling to join in the operation of route 236 (South Hampstead and Farnborough), providing 16 buses along with General providing 16 covered-top NSs from Nunhead. Route 147, which had continued to operate even during the winter although on a widened headway since 1927, was at the same time taken over by Catford garage on Sundays.

During summer Sundays certain buses on the 47 route were extended to Knockholt Pound under the number 147. O 45, a Catford bus, is seen in the summer of 1930.

As Catford only worked the 36 on weekdays its buses were available for use on special Sunday services. In July 1929 O 44 was working on the long 236A route between South Hampstead and Bromley Common.

During the height of the summer when the weather was favourable, and more especially on August bank holiday which in those days fell at the beginning of the month, many of the busiest routes out into the surrounding countryside were very heavily supplemented by the use of spare and extra buses. For example, it is noted that on 3rd August 1925, fifty-four TS3As ran from Croydon on the 59 (Camden Town and Reigate) and 34 on the 159 (Camden Town and Godstone). Consequently, route 75 was operated entirely by Catford with 34 buses, so that only 22 were left for the 12E. The General made up this difference on the 12E by providing buses from Streatham garage.

The following table summarises the schedules for high summer 1929.

ALLOCATION OF SCHEDULED BUSES ON SUNDAYS FROM 3rd JULY 1929

Route	Details	Garage	Type	Number
1B	Willesden – Chislehurst	TL	PE	17
12	Shepherds Bush – South Croydon	TL	PE	35
		ED	*NS	9
21A	Wood Green – Sidcup	TL	PE	11
		AD	S	16
		SP	S	12
36	West Kilburn – Hither Green	TB	PE	36
47A	Shoreditch – Farnborough	TB	PE	16
		D	*NS	16 (MET livery)
49C	Shepherds Bush – Lewisham	TC	PE	18
		AK	K	17
58	Camden Town – Chipstead Valley Road	TC	PE	15
		AK	*NS	15
59	Camden Town – Reigate	TC	PE	20
59A	Camden Town – Coulsdon	TC	PE	22
75	Godstone – Woolwich	TL	PE	9
		TC	PE	10
75D	Caterham – Woolwich	TL	PE	7
		TC	PE	10
78A	Shoreditch – Dulwich	TL	PE	19
109	Penge – Eltham	TB	†PE	11
		SP	†K	3
112	Park Royal – Lower Sydenham	TL	PE	10
		M	S	10
136	West Kilburn – Bromley Common	TL	PE	22
147	Shoreditch – Knockholt Pound	TL	PE	8
213	Plumstead Common – Westerham Hill	TB	PE	16
236	South Hampstead – Farnborough	TL	PE	16
		AH	K	16
289A	Plumstead Common – Bromley Common	TB	PE	10

*Covered-top   †Single-deck

7 Leading up to the LPTB 1930-1933

Even as the new decade started it was clear that Tilling's bus operation would not survive in the capital for many more years. Politics had come to play a large part in the transport of the public. After so many years of harmony within the London Omnibus Pool, the last few years were characterised by increasing discord as Tilling found that they had little say in what was bound to happen. Nonetheless, at the start of 1930, Tilling found themselves operating a number of important and very lucrative routes, and even in this time of economic stringency the shareholders could not be displeased with the profits. The fleet itself was showing its age, and once the decision had been taken to abandon the petrol-electrics the way was open for a major fleet modernisation programme.

Herbert Morrison, Minister of Transport in the Labour government of 1929, had seen a need to reform what he saw as the fragmented transport services of the Metropolis. On 2nd December, he announced proposals for a comprehensive solution. These involved unification under public control; management by a non-political body; participation by the main-line railways without transfer of ownership; and a self-supporting unsubsidised system to be run as a commercial enterprise. Sir William McLintock was charged with the duty of drawing up the details, and although Tilling were deeply suspicious of his investigations into their finances, they were later to comment that at least he had concerned himself with their affairs, while later arrangements were made with the minimum of consultation. The bill as published on 13th March 1931 allowed the shareholders in the Underground Group and the Metropolitan Companies to be issued with transport stock in the new undertaking. Tilling and the remaining independent companies would get transport stock and/or cash, the amount being agreed by negotiation or, failing that, by an arbitration tribunal. Tilling were somewhat galled to be treated in the same way as the most opportunist independents after their loyal years in the Pool. They themselves had had to face competition from independents on their busiest routes, especially those through central London such as the 21, 36, 47 and 59. Although in August 1931 the Labour government was defeated, the incoming 'National' government proposed to continue where the previous government had left off. J.F. Heaton, chairman of Thomas Tilling at the time, wanted the whole question re-examined but his was a lone voice in the wilderness. He agreed with the need for a co-ordinated scheme for London, but he never had the opportunity to put forward his own views on this officially.

Royal Assent was given to the London Passenger Transport Act on 13th April 1933 and the London Omnibus Pool was dissolved. The new Board came into being on 1st July, but by this time Tilling were in acrimonious dispute over the terms and it was some weeks and many words later before their London bus operation ceased. They were taken over eventually on 1st October 1933.

Returning to 1929, it is noted that at the end of that year the LGOC had about 2,000 covered-top NS type buses in service, 400 of them fitted with pneumatic tyres. About 1,700 open-topped buses of the K and S types and a few NSs with open-tops were still in use, but these were rapidly being withdrawn as new buses became available. The LT type six-wheeled AEC Renowns were in course of delivery. On the other hand Tilling's fleet of 352 double deckers were all open toppers with solid tyres of the TS3A and TS7 type, having entered service between 1921 and 1924. A total of 316 were licensed to work on weekdays on 17 routes with approximatley 320 in operation on a similar number of routes on Sunday.

But a change was on the way. Tilling, having experimented with the covered-top Tilling-Stevens TS17A, finding its performance disappointing, and also with an AEC Regent, decided to abandon petrol-electric traction in favour of petrol-engined vehicles. Therefore in December 1929, the Company placed an order with AEC for 136 Regent chassis with bodies to be built either by Tilling themselves at their Camberwell, Lewisham or Brighton works, or by Dodson Ltd to Tilling's own design. In order to obtain the maximum passenger capacity, a covered-top open-staircase body was designed to seat 52 passengers (25 inside, and 27 on the top deck).

These buses were numbered in a new series separating them from other motor vehicles, beginning at 6001. The first 12 were for use in Brighton, so the first London bus was numbered 6013. Registrations were reserved with the London Registration Department, being GJ2001-2100 followed by GK1001-1036. Another 62 Regent chassis were subsequently ordered so as to make a total of 186 AEC Regent covered-top buses, sufficient to replace all 166 TS3A buses in the London fleet as well as the 20 former Timpson vehicles. These were numbered 6137 to 6198 and registered as GK6237-6298. Further Regents of the same type were added to the Brighton fleet.

The first bus for London, 6013, was sent to Bromley garage and entered service on 27th June 1930 working duty TB3 on route 36, which Tilling regarded as their prime route. Within the next month sufficient of the new vehicles were delivered to complete the full allocation of 33 buses from Bromley garage on that route. Initially these buses had the style of route number shown by a stencil plate in a box on the driver's canopy and destination and route boards, similar to the O type buses. The extreme destination boards were however slotted inside the top deck front windows. The front registration

By June 1930 when this picture of number 835 (XF 9820) was taken at Peckham Rye, the bus was running as TL16 on the 78A, having been transferred from route 36 in exchange for a TS7.

Also seen at Peckham Rye in June 1930 is O 58 working on the 112E route from East Acton to Lower Sydenham, Bell Green. The eight buses O 56-63 had operated on the Lower Sydenham route 112 ever since 1924. The TS7 can be compared with the older TS3A type in the previous picture.

The first twelve of the new AEC Regents went to Brighton, so number 6013 was the first to run in London, doing so in June 1930. Here we see the second bus, 6014, standing at West Kilburn in front of a Tilling-Stevens. The route board and service number are better placed and a new style of fleetname has been adopted.

number was therefore fitted below the radiator. A significant change took place with all later new Regent buses as the route number boxes were dispensed with following the fitting of a roller blind box showing extreme destination as well as the service number. A reduced-size route board was fitted beneath, similar fittings appearing at the rear of the bus. The front registration number reverted to the normal Tilling position in the centre of the roof of the driver's canopy. The earlier buses were then soon changed to this revised style.

August and September 1930 saw further new buses being sent to Bromley garage so that the allocation of 27 buses on route 47 could be replaced together with three on that route from Catford garage. On Monday 27th October, the first Regent buses from Catford garage started to operate route 36, followed by a further 14 to complete the allocation. Eleven of these new buses were then put on to route 12A, also from Catford garage. When the winter schedules were introduced on 5th November 1930, six of the new covered-top buses were taken off the Bromley allocation on route 47, reducing it to 21 vehicles and these were transferred to Catford garage where they were put on to route 146A (Lewisham and Keston) replacing a similar number of General buses. To balance this, six TS7s working on route 136 (West Kilburn to Bromley Common) were transferred from Catford to Bromley garage.

It had been a long while since Croydon had operated new buses, but the first Regents from that garage were put on to route 59A on 6th December 1930. By early 1931, 25 Regent buses were allocated to the garage, enabling 15 buses to work the 12A as well as ten for the 59A. At the same time, new buses continued to enter service from Catford garage, and 14 were soon working service 112A. Apart from nine more which also went to Catford for the 112E, the modernisation of the fleet at Croydon began in earnest. From mid-May 1931, the 59A had 23 covered-top buses and the 59B had 25. These totals included 15 Regents taken from the 12A route, which had to revert to petrol-electrics for a time. It will be recalled that in 1922 when the new TS3As were entering service, the swap was in reverse with the 59A losing the new buses temporarily to the 12A. The last 23 Regent buses arrived during June 1931 and 15 were used to re-equip the 12A. The other nine went to Catford and were placed on route 1C, the last new bus of all, 6198, being put into service on 1st July 1931.

One bus, number 6130, was loaned to Tilling at Brighton from 30th January 1931 but returned to London in mid-June when it was allocated to Croydon. The 186 AEC Regents replaced all the TS3 and TS3A types which had progressively been withdrawn and sold. The first of all to go were the 20 buses ex-Timpson, and thus route 289A was operated by TS7s displaced from route 36. Other surplus TS7s from Bromley then passed to Catford to replace TS3As on routes such as the 78A and some then went on to Croydon, the first O types to be operated from that garage, working routes such as 59B or 75. Gradually, as the new buses entered service,

No. 6115, one of the first Regents to be allocated to Croydon garage, is seen near Purley tram terminus on its way to Camden Town whilst XH 9299, a TS3A on the 59A on the way to Coulsdon, passes in the other direction. The Regents had by this time been fitted with a roller blind box showing extreme destination and service number with a reduced size route board underneath.

the remaining TS3As which had rendered such yeoman service were withdrawn and the TS7s were reallocated as necessary. By 1st July 1931, the Tilling fleet was distributed as follows:

	AEC Regent	TS7	(TS7 in service)
Bromley	54	35	(23)
Catford	70	90	(81)
Croydon	62	41	(25)

At that time the following services were still worked wholly or partly by open-top petrol-electrics: 136, 289 (Bromley), 1C, 21A, 136, 75, 78A (Catford), Sunday 49C, 59B, 75 (Croydon). All Tilling services were approved for covered-top operation with the exception of routes 49C, 75 and 136, where the problems were overhanging trees or lamp posts that needed resiting, mainly in the Borough of Lewisham. All the other routes except the 36 had covered-top NSs working on them at times. The NSs on the 12 group of routes were replaced by new LTs during 1931.

Meanwhile, during 1930 and 1931 certain route changes affecting Tilling working had taken place. First, on Sunday 5th January 1930, six buses from Catford garage were on Sundays placed on Croydon route 58 (Camden Town and Chipstead Valley Road), the buses entering service at Kennington after proceeding from Catford garage by way of the 36 road. On 29th January, routes 112A and 112C were extended from Park Royal to Harlesden (Willesden Junction Station), as was the 112 on Sundays. There was no change in the Tilling allocation of 14 buses on weekdays and ten on Sundays.

The reduced style of route board showing only four lines of detail, similar to that carried by the Regents, was adopted for the remaining TS7 petrol-electrics as can be seen in this picture of O 30 at Wood Green on the 21A service.

Regent number 6158 from Croydon garage, proceeding to Oxford Circus on the 12A service.

During the summer of 1929 the twelve single-deck TS7 buses on route 109 had been fitted with pneumatic tyres. This picture of XW 9894 shows that the buses still bore General livery.

Below In March 1930 the twelve TS7 single deckers were licensed in the name of Tilling and repainted into full Tilling livery. The change is seen with O 171 standing outside the 'Crooked Billet' at Penge in 1932.

Gradually during the summer of 1929 the 12 single-deck TS7s on route 109 had been converted to pneumatic tyres. They still bore GENERAL fleetnames, but on 12th March 1930 they were licensed in the name of Tilling and repainted in Tilling livery — the same as the double-deck TS7 buses. From the same date the route was speeded up with a journey time reduced from 66 minutes to 52, and so it was possible to withdraw the LGOC allocation and cover the entire route with 11 Tilling buses (four K types from Nunhead garage continued to work the 109A — Penge and Bromley — on Saturdays).

The summer Sunday programme came into force on 13th April 1930 with Tilling putting 17 buses on the 1B to Chislehurst as well as another 13 on the 1C (Willesden and Lewisham). The usual additional buses were put on to the 75 to Godstone and the 146 to Westerham Hill.

One variation that year was the extension of the 289A to Green Street Green as 289. Tilling withdrew from the 112 on Sundays and instead increased the Catford allocation on the 58 to 15. Starting on 4th June the limited weekday service on route 147 was withdrawn, as the section of road between Green Street Green and Knockholt Pound was covered by a new service introduced by East Surrey Traction Company, numbered 31, which operated between Sevenoaks and Chelsfield. The 147 continued to run on Sundays.

The single-deck service 109 was revised from 3rd September when the headway to Eltham was widened to every 15 minutes and increased to a joint 7½-minute frequency between Penge and Chislehurst with the introduction of a short working under number 109D. The allocation was 11 Tillings and two LGOC T type (ED).

O 86 stands outside a still familiar part of Catford garage and is getting ready to join the 75D route at Catford Town Hall and then to go southwards to Caterham Valley.

Below This view of a Regent standing outside Catford garage shows that the front of the garage has changed little over the years. The bus, on a Sunday working from this garage, must make a long journey via Kennington to join the 159C route to South Croydon.

With the introduction of the winter programme from 8th October 1930, some changes took place in the 59 group working. The ten buses that ran the Monday to Friday operation between Camden Town and Reigate were withdrawn and replaced by a new East Surrey route numbered 459, running every 30 minutes from West Croydon to Reigate over the same route as 59 via Wray Common. Tilling continued the weekday operation with 23 buses on the 59A to Coulsdon and 30 on the 59B (Camden Town and South Croydon). The 59 continued to work to Reigate on Saturdays and Sundays when the 459 did not run. Commencing on 11th October, six buses from Bromley garage worked on Sundays on route 75, so that all three Tilling garages were to be found running on the route during that winter season.

When the Willesden and Chislehurst route returned

for the summer Sundays on 5th April 1931, it was numbered 1 instead of 1B, again operated by 17 petrol-electrics. The 59 to Reigate was withdrawn on Saturdays as well, being replaced by the 459. Changes in Sunday operation from 24th May resulted in the LGOC taking over the 49C and 22 Croydon buses working instead on route 159C (Oxford Circus and South Croydon via Thornton Heath). The LGOC replaced the 15 Tilling STs on the 58, which were then operated on the 47 for the summer season. With the winter programme on 11th October, Tilling came back on to 49C with 18 petrol-electrics and the LGOC provided 17 NSs from Streatham garage. The 159C was divided between the two garages, 11 each from Catford and Croydon. LGOC referred to Tilling's Regents as ST type in line with their own AEC Regents.

Route 254 was introduced in 1931 to serve the new housing estate in the Croham Heights area and because of a low bridge at South Croydon had to be worked by open-top buses from Croydon garage. O 159 was one of the TS7s fitted with pneumatic tyres and is on the return journey to the 'Swan and Sugar Loaf'.

On 4th November 1931, the 112 on Sundays and 112E weekdays were withdrawn between East Dulwich and Lower Sydenham. As replacement, part of the 78A service was extended from East Dulwich to West Wickham via Forest Hill and Lower Sydenham as number 78. This extended route was jointly worked with the LGOC with 12 LT type from Nunhead garage and 13 Tilling buses from Catford. Owing to a low railway bridge in Elmers End Road, only covered-top buses could be used on this service and these became available by using the nine AEC Regents previously on the 112E, with four off the 1C. The 78A Shoreditch and Dulwich with 13 Tillings continued with the TS7 type. On Sunday the LGOC operated the 78 with 20 LTs and Tilling put 19 TS7s on the 78A.

A new Tilling route began on Wednesday 16th December 1931. This was the 254, between South Croydon (Swan and Sugar Loaf) and Croham Heights (Brent Road) worked by two buses from Croydon garage. Owing to a very low bridge in Croham Road, near South Croydon Station, only open-top petrol-electric buses could be used and conductors were instructed to warn passengers on the top deck to remain seated whilst passing under the bridge. Buses were also prohibited from passing each other in the narrow section of Croham Road. This route originated in a private bus service put on by Richard Costains, the builders, who had developed the estate in the Selsdon area since 1925. One Tilling bus had been hired from Croydon garage by Costains since 18th May 1929. Although a summons was issued against Costains in October 1929 for unlawfully plying for hire on this private bus service, it was satisfactorily settled and the service continued until replaced by the 254. The new service commenced at a 10-minute interval, but the headway was widened to every 15 minutes in January 1932. It was extended from Brent Road to Selsdon on 15th March 1933 with the addition

of one more O type. A number of Croham Valley residents rather resented the presence of Selsdon passengers on their local bus.

Commencing 30th December the 136 was extended from Bromley Common to Southborough with the same 20 buses being used. There was also a revision in the 59 group with a decreased service on the 59B in the slack hours, its allocation being reduced to 12, and Tilling placed 18 STs on to route 58 thus working this route on weekdays as well. The LGOC added six NSs from Old Kent Road (P) and the 58 was increased to a ten-minute headway, and together with the 59A provided a joint five-minute service between Camden Town and Coulsdon. The 59B being mainly a peak hour operation, it reverted to open-top petrol-electrics.

The first part of the summer programme began early in 1932 as Good Friday fell on 25th March. Tilling buses again worked through to Chislehurst on Sundays as the 1 using open-toppers, but the 1C between Willesden and Lewisham had STs on Sunday from Catford. On weekdays, seven of the 20 Tilling vehicles were scheduled to be STs. The Sunday Godstone journeys on the 75 were introduced again, but this time the 78 and 78A were left to LGOC once more. Another revision to the 112A route on weekdays took place on 11th May 1932, when it was withdrawn between Harlesden and Park Royal. It now ran as 112A between Park Royal and East Dulwich and with the 112C (East Acton and East Dulwich) the weekday allocation became quite complicated. For the 112A, Camberwell provided eight NSs, Nunhead ten LTs, Shepherds Bush 11 LTs and Catford five STs. The 112C used six LTs each from Nunhead, Elmers End and Shepherds Bush, whilst Catford ran only six STs and six open-top TS7s. The 112C was mainly a peak hour service and the displaced STs from the 112C and seven STs off the 1C enabled 13 covered-top buses to be put on to the 78A.

Although Tilling had replaced its own fleet of Tilling-Stevens TS3A type with the new covered-top Regents, the jointly owned TS7s also needed replacement, though by this time 64 of the TS7 fleet had been transferred to Tilling ownership. The LGOC therefore decided to replace the 102 remaining in their ownership by modern buses. This resulted in an order being placed in the early part of 1932 for a number of AEC Regent chassis. As the Ministry of Transport had increased the permitted length for a four-wheeled bus, it was the later Regent chassis which were to be purchased. This initial order was for 80 chassis, which was actually placed before LGOC ordered its own examples of what was to become the numerous STL class. As Tilling were so fuel-consumption conscious, the engine was downrated noticeably and a number of other modifications were required. They even denied their staff the use of self starters, drivers being expected to swing the handle in the now rather-outdated fashion.

Eighty-four bodies were built by Tilling themselves, allowing for four float spares so that the overhaul system already in use by both LGOC and Tilling could continue. Fifty-six seats were divided between 30 in the upper saloon and 26 in the lower. The staircase was enclosed, and full roller blinds were used in the indicators rather than the boards and strip roller blinds on Tilling's own buses. Being General-owned, these buses were numbered in their STL series, but as the first 50 of this type had been ordered, the new Tilling buses were numbered STL 51 to STL 130. As the anticipated order for the last 22 needed to replace the remaining LGOC owned petrol-electrics was not made, STLs 131-152 were never built. The bodies designed by Tilling turned out to be more curvaceous than those early members of LGOC's STL class and the unusual Tilling three-window layout at the front upper deck was retained. The interiors were regarded as quite handsome and less

Top **In 1932 the LGOC purchased twelve AEC Regals to replace the single-deck petrol-electrics on the 109 service. Numbered in the LGOC T class, the fleet number T 311 is seen by the base of the radiator. The photograph was taken at Penge in September 1932. Above The LGOC assisted in the operation of the 109 service with some six-wheeled LTs from Elmers End garage. LT 1188 has a very limited blind display as compared with the Tilling T type.**

spartan than the General's new buses of the time, but although the bodies were a little more robust than the STs, yet sagging, distorted waistrails and movement in the joints caused a great deal of trouble quite early in the life of some the examples.

The LGOC also purchased 12 AEC Regal chassis to replace the TS7 single-deck buses on route 109. Tilling-built 28-seat bodies were used, and the vehicles were placed in LGOC's T class as T307-318. The first of these new single deckers were put into service on the 109 on 18th August 1932, and the last on 1st October. The remarkably square frontal appearance and larger indicator box at the front were especially noteworthy features. They were painted in full Tilling livery.

For demonstration purposes the first Tilling STL was fitted with blinds reading 1C LEWISHAM, though it is doubtful if this new type ever ran on this service. The fleet number ST 837 had been painted on the front dumbirons before the LGOC decided to include the bus in the STL class. It then became STL 51.

The first chassis of the STL class was delivered to Tilling on 13th October 1932 and received its new body almost immediately. It was at first given the number ST 837 to follow on from General's own ST class, but it was changed to STL 51 before it entered service.

Route 36 was again chosen for the new bus when the first STL was put into service on 29th October 1932, this time from Catford garage. Twelve of the new buses, STLs 51-61/3, were delivered by mid-December and completed the Catford allocation for the route. The next 19 STLs went to Bromley garage, being part of the 36 allocation, and by the middle of February 1933, STLs 64-81/5 were in service. Another seven arrivals that month (STLs 86/8-93) went to Catford, six going on the 112A route and the last one on the 12A. Soon afterwards, however, all seven were put on to the 12A to complete the Catford allocation, the 112A reverting to ST type. STL 62 was the first of the new type to be sent to Croydon at the end of December 1932, and it entered service as

TC1 on route 59A. Nineteen further STLs went on the 59A during February and March 1933 to complete the allocation, being STLs 82-4/7, 94/5/7-105/7-10. The last 22 of the STL type were licensed between the middle of April and 30th June, and 16 of these (STLs 96, 106/11-22/9/30) were allocated to Croydon for service 58. Six, STLs 123-8, replaced O types on the 112C from Catford during June. These buses were retained on these routes for the remainder of the period of the Tilling régime, although towards the end of that time eight of them (STLs 114-121) were taken off route 58 and sent to Bromley for route 36 in exchange for STs. Also, STLs 125-128 were replaced on the 112C by STs and they were sent to Croydon where they ran on the 75 route on weekdays and the 49C on Sundays. There was not a lot of change in the Sunday operation of these STLs, but during the summer season of 1933, route 147 used seven from Bromley and the 59 had a full allocation of 21 from Croydon.

Left **The 112C was a peak hour route from East Acton to Dulwich (The Plough). O 145, having completed its rush hour work, is running back to Catford garage but waits in Lordship Lane for the return of the driver.** Right **STL 104, a Croydon bus, lays over at Camden Town before setting out on the long 59A route to Coulsdon. The use of the small number box above the entrance was abandoned by London Transport and replaced by the small stencil at the base of the rear downstairs window.**

The normal weekday service 1C, Willesden and Lewisham, was one of the last routes to regularly use solid tyred open-top petrol-electrics. O 29 is standing at the Lewisham terminus in Rennell Street during the summer of 1933.

A rear view of STL 105 soon after it had entered service from Croydon garage on the 59A route. This picture, taken at Streatham in 1933, shows the original position of the rear registration number and the Metropolitan Police licence plate, both of which London Transport eventually moved to the inner bulkhead by the rear entrance.

The General-owned STL buses thus replaced 80 of the TS7s, which were withdrawn and sold between November 1932 and August 1933. A further reduction in the fleet of O types occurred owing to the diminishing number of buses required for service. This was due to the speeding up of London bus services following the fitting of pneumatic tyres and to the use of higher capacity and more powerful vehicles. Tilling's fleet had been maintained at the agreed maximum of 316 buses in service until October 1932 but a gradual reduction had taken place since then. For example, route 36 had been reduced from 48 to 41 buses, the 59 group from 55 to 48 buses, and when the 12A was speeded up from 1st

February, four Catford buses were taken off. Therefore during 1933, a total of 36 TS7s were taken out of service and stored. In April 1933, five of the Regents in the Brighton fleet were found to be surplus to requirements, transferred to London and sent to Catford garage. These were numbered 6225/7/8/30/6, and this allowed five more TS7s to be withdrawn and stored. The result was that by July 1933 only 45 open-top Tilling-Stevens buses remained in service, 15 at Croydon garage, and 30 at Catford. During 1932 and 1933, twenty-five of these had been fitted with pneumatic tyres, being O 32/4/5/7/9-42/ 5/8/50/1/4/7/60/3/6/9/70/2/81/96, 150/5/9. This enabled them to be used more effectively with the newer buses.

Left This bus, 6227, was one of the five Regents transferred to London from the Brighton fleet in April 1933. It is seen as it passes Lewisham Park Dental Hospital when working on the 146B route to Downe in summer 1933. Right A rear view of 6225, another bus from the Brighton fleet, shown in London while on Private Hire. Some points to note are the fitting of a rear bumper, tried out on some buses at the time, and the used ticket box. Since coming to London the Metropolitan Police licence number 7392 has been allocated.

The introduction of the new STLs meant a certain amount of reallocation so as to replace the O types with covered-top buses. The last route to be approved for covered-tops was the 136 in February 1933. By mid-1933, the 21A, 75, 78A, 136, and 289 had all received covered-top buses, and curiously it was the 1C which was the last to change. Route 254 remained open-top but it had special problems with the low bridge.

The first part of 1933 was quiet as far as route changes were concerned. On 12th April the 75D was renumbered 75, as the summer extension to Godstone did not take place again. Green Line had taken over as the means to visit the beauty spots in various parts of London's country. Route 1 was again extended on summer Sundays, however, this time beyond Chislehurst to Green Street Green. Twenty TS7s were required. On 31st May, the single-deck route 109 was extended from Eltham to Welling (Guy Earl of Warwick). Also on that day, certain buses on route 146A were extended from Keston to Downe High Street as 146B. One of the last route changes of all as far as Tilling were concerned came on 23rd August when their contribution on the 21A was reduced to 21 STs, and five O types were put instead on a short-working 20D, a peak hour working between Wood Green and Old Kent Road. The very last alteration to Tilling services took place on 1st October, the day of the takeover, when route 59 operated to Reigate for the last time. Technically, this was the only day that LPTB operated to Reigate using red buses of the Central area.

Many Croydon garage buses were operated on Sundays on the 49C between Shepherds Bush and Lewisham. O 51, a TS7 that had been fitted with pneumatics, is on the Rennell Street stand in front of a Regent on the 146.

Regent No. 6164, working as TL13 on the 78 route, is standing in Lordship Lane, Dulwich opposite the 'Grove Hotel' whilst on the way to West Wickham in 1933.

Croydon was able to allocate covered-top buses to the 49C on Sundays and 6111 is waiting at Rennell Street before going on to Shepherds Bush. The stand is shared in this photograph by a General ST.

The London Passenger Transport Board had come into being on 1st July 1933, the date on which the LGOC was taken over, but there was a delay as far as Tilling were concerned as they were in bitter opposition over the valuation of assets. A compromise had meant that Tilling was to retain the Wren Road and Pelican Yard factories, but the Board acquired the Bull Yard and the Obelisk Works. Chassis overhauling would be concentrated at the Bull Yard whilst bodies would be dealt with at the Obelisk Works. All body construction at the Lewisham Works would cease. It was just about to undertake the construction of the last four STL bodies for float purposes in October, which were thus never built by Tilling.

The control and ownership of 369 buses, of which forty-one were delicensed, passed to the Board. The total staffs involved in the transfer were 865 drivers, 860 conductors, 234 coach-building staff, 225 inside staff and 198 engineering personnel. The three garages, Catford, Bromley and Croydon, were already LGOC property and so had passed to LPTB. Of the buses, 255 were Tilling's own and 114 were the remainder of the 'float' of buses owned by the LGOC and worked on its behalf by Tilling. Notices of the transfer to LPTB had appeared on the fare boards from September 25th. Outwardly there was not much to be seen on the vehicles on 1st October apart from the name of the new legal owner on the lower panels of the buses. The actual operating fleet at the time of transfer consisted of 80 STLs, 191 STs, 12 single-deck Ts and 45 petrol-electric O type. The first Tilling bus to appear in GENERAL livery was 6081 ex-Catford on 19th October. It was followed by 6092, 6083, 6084 and 6086 with Tilling fleet numbers on the dumb iron. No. 6101, in service 25th October, was the first with a number in gold on the bonnet and cab side. These Tilling Regents were then given ST fleet numbers in the LPTB series, viz ST 837 to ST 1027. The STL and T types were already numbered and the STL numbers were removed

from the dumb iron to the bonnet on Sunday 15th October. In due course the buses were repainted into the standard LPTB livery, although for a time the fleetname of GENERAL was in use pending the adoption of that of LONDON TRANSPORT some months later. The front registration numbers were moved from the Tilling position on the canopy to beneath the radiator.

Above By the end of October 1933 the Tilling Regents were given ST fleet numbers in place of the original Tilling numbers. This picture shows ST 872 (formerly 6048) at Victoria when working on the 136 route. The LGOC style route board with white letters on black background has replaced the Tilling boards.

Left The STL fleet numbers were removed from the dumbirons and painted in gold on the bonnets or cab sides in LPTB fashion in mid-October. Apart from STL 64 on the cab side, this bus shows no other sign of change of ownership.

The rear registration number on the STLs was changed from the illuminated box in the centre of the back below the indicator blinds to a position above the rear bulkhead similar to the General STs. The nearside rear route number box on the STLs was removed and replaced by the LPTB stencil mounted in the nearside rearmost window. Certain other modifications took place with the STLs during the next three years which were generally improvements, such as the fitting of starter motors. Men at Bromley garage had gone on strike in October 1934 because they considered that the fitment was not taking place rapidly enough.

At the time of transfer to LPTB there were 280 buses scheduled for weekday operation, including 80 STL which were distributed as follows: 12A (TL) 7, 112A (TL) 1, 36 (TB) 28, 36 (TL) 12, 58 (TC) 8, 59A (TC) 20 and 75 (TC) 4. Thirty-four petrol-electrics were 1C (TL) 13, 20D (TL) 5, 112C (TL) 5, 59B (TC) 8 and 254 (TC) 3. All the other Tilling routes were worked by STs. The allocation of vehicles was as follows:

TL	O type:	O 21-41/5/50/7, 161/3-6
	ST type:	ST 838-41/3-7/50-2/5/8/65/6/75/9/82/6/7/ 9/91, 905-24/7/8/30/1/4/5/8/40/2-5/7/9/ 52/5/8/61/3/7-73/6/7/80/1/3/5/7-92/4/6/8/ 9, 1000-4/8/9/12-6/8/9/22.
	STL type:	STL 51-61/3, 86/8-93.
TB	O type:	Nil
	ST type:	ST 837/42/8/9/53/4/6/7/9-61/3/4/7/72/4/ 7/81/4/5/90/2/4/5/7-904/25/9/66/74/84/6/ 93/5, 1005/10/7.
	STL type:	STL 64-81/5, 114/5/9/21.
	T type:	T 307-18
TC	O type:	O 48/51/4/60/3/6/9/70/2/81/94, 150/5/9/ 62.
	ST type:	ST 862/8-71/3/6/8/80/3/8/93/6, 926/32/3/ 6/7/9/41/6/8/50/1/3/4/6/7/9/60/2/4/5/75/ 8/9/82/97, 1006/7/11/20/1.
	STL type:	STL 62/82-4/7/94-113/6-8/20/2-30.

Note: STLs 116-8, 20/2 were transferred from TC to TB on 4th October 1933.

Above **This picture of ST 916 at Farnborough in October 1933 whilst on route 47A shows that it had been repainted in LPTB livery with GENERAL fleetname, yet it still had a Tilling style route board and the registration number in its original position.**

Left **As the legal lettering on the side of this STL indicates, the days of the Tilling fleetname on London buses are numbered.**

8 Operation by London Transport 1933-1939

Although Thomas Tilling's London bus services had been taken over by London Transport on 1st October 1933, operation was continued in much the same way for nearly six years. Tilling's fleet of 191 ST and 80 STL type buses was retained at the former Tilling garages, Bromley, Catford and Croydon. Also, by June 1939, twelve of the former Tilling routes were still being operated by buses bearing the familiar TB, TC, and TL codes. Even the allocations were much the same and many buses were still working the long garage journeys from Bromley to Catford or from Catford garage to Forest Hill and Dulwich. This pattern of operation was destined to change dramatically three or four months later after the outbreak of the Second World War.

There had been some changes, as London Transport had found it necessary to allocate certain new routes to each of the three garages as time went by, and a number of extra buses were brought in — many of these being new petrol-engined STLs but also some former General STs.

One of the first moves by London Transport upon taking over Tilling's services was to replace the remaining O type petrol-electrics and it was only ten days after takeover that two former LGOC buses, STs 117/71, were sent to Catford garage, followed by ST 168 on 11th October. By the end of November at least 27 LPTB STs had entered service at the garage. They were all fresh from overhaul. Therefore by 29th November routes 1c, 20d and 112c were all operated by STs from Catford whilst Croydon's route 59b was converted from O type by the transfer of ex-Tilling STs from Catford, which were replaced by more from the Board. The petrol electrics continued on route 254 at Croydon for a few months until on 29th January 1934, five open-top AEC Regents acquired from an Independent, C.H. Pickup of Dulwich, were transferred to Croydon. These buses, STLs 553-557, were very useful in working under the low bridge but as only three were needed for this route one or more were to be found on the 59b. All the O type were withdrawn and sold, several becoming showmen's vehicles. Nine were converted by the LPTB for use as tower wagons for the Tramway and Trolleybus Division.

Five open-top AEC Regents were obtained by London Transport from C.H. Pickup of Dulwich and numbered STL 553-57. In January 1934 they were transferred to Croydon garage for use on the 254 route, replacing the TS7s. STL 554 is seen at the Selsdon terminus.

A slight change of operation took place on 13th December 1933 when four ex-Tilling STs from the Croydon allocation of the 12A service were used as peak hour extras on route 179, no doubt prior to working to Oxford Circus on their normal duties. The 179 ran between Croydon and Shirley via Addiscombe Road and was otherwise operated by five NS type from ED garage.

The first reallocation of former Tilling buses undertaken by London Transport took place with the 36 and 136 routes on 31st January 1934. The 36 changed from Catford 12, Bromley 29 to Catford 28, Bromley 15, whilst the 136 changed from Catford 12, Bromley 6 to Bromley 18. The 36 had previously been worked by STLs and the 136 by STs, but the alteration meant ten STLs working on the 136 with ten STs needed to complete Catford's working on the 36. This changed on 14th February when STLs 64-72/6 were transferred from

Bromley to Catford to complete the allocation of STLs on the 36. However, the 36 allocation changed again on 11th April when Catford's quota on the route was reduced to 16 and Bromley increased to 27, and to retain the STL coverage on the route 12 STLs were transferred from Catford to Bromley, these being STLs 51/2/4-61/3,86.

The first additional working to be undertaken by Catford garage occurred on 17th January 1934 when seven buses, former LGOC STs, were transferred to operate the 536C route between Highgate and Elmers End. The 536 route had been started in January 1925 by the City Motor Omnibus Company Ltd of Peckham in company with United Omnibus Company, also of Peckham, and ran from Highgate to Brockley via Oxford Circus, Victoria and New Cross. It soon became a very successful route that penetrated Tilling territory and was in competition with the 36 route from Victoria to New Cross. Birch Bros Ltd also joined in this operation. The route was extended on 15th April 1925 from Brockley along Stanstead Road to Catford to terminate at Southend Village (Tiger's Head). Two years later it was further extended through Beckenham to Elmers End. Subsequently, on 25th May 1930, the Sunday operation ran on further to West Wickham. All three companies at first operated open-top Leyland buses and by 1927 forty buses were working the 536 to Elmers End; three Birch, seven United and 30 City. All three companies had similar brown and cream livery. The route was worked on a regular schedule based on the Tilling pattern using duty or running numbers from C1 upwards and the same bus was usually retained on the same duty each day unless replaced by a spare vehicle. Upon the extension to Elmers End, Birch's three buses ran as C1-C3, United's were C11, 16, 21, 26, 31 and 36 and City occupied the intervening numbers to C35. During peak hours, three extra City and one United were operated. United was the first to regularly operate covered-top buses on the 536, having purchased seven Leyland Titans in 1930/1, followed by Birch Bros, also with Titans. Eventually, City purchased 12 Leyland Titans in 1931/2, but City also operated six six-wheeled Leylands rebuilt from open-top buses and ten six-wheeled Guys. Finally they obtained three six-wheeled Leyland Titanics in March 1933, so quite a mixed fleet was to be found on the 536. The seven United Titans plus one open-top Leyland were acquired by London Transport on 1st November 1933 but they continued to operate until 17th January 1934, when the United buses were withdrawn and replaced by eight ex-LGOC STs

allocated to Catford garage. They operated on the same timings as United in company with the City and Birch buses on 536C on weekdays to Elmers End and 536 on Sundays to West Wickham. Birch Bros' fleet was taken over by London Transport on 21st February 1934 and the three buses on the 536 were replaced by ST buses working from Chalk Farm garage (CF). In the summer of 1934 these STs were replaced by new STLs. The route was renumbered 137 on 3rd October and eventually on 7th November 1934 the City's fleet of buses was taken over by the LPTB and these too were replaced by buses working from Catford garage. For this operation, 30 new petrol-engined STLs were supplied to Catford (STLs 559, 61/4/76/7/9/80/6-99, 600-8). They were in fact among the last petrol-engined buses new to the Board. From 7th November the 137 allocation was 37 STL or ST from Catford on weekdays and 38 on Sundays together with 14 STs from Old Kent Road (P).

Although the former Timpson route 213 (Plumstead Common and Westerham Hill) had ceased as a regular Sunday operation on 4th October 1931, it had been retained for an early morning journey to Westerham Hill. The reason for this was that East Surrey (later London General Country Services) did not run a sufficiently early duty on route 410 into Bromley. So a 213 bus ran from Lewisham at 6.45am for Westerham Hill and returned from there at 8.07am bound for Plumstead Common. From 31st January 1934, this early morning journey from Lewisham was numbered 289E and the return to Plumstead Common as 289. Starting early in 1932 a similar early-morning journey was operated by buses on route 47 to Green Street Green on weekdays. A bus left Shoreditch at 6am and returned from Green Street Green at 7.35am. Times varied by a few minutes over the years.

When the summer Sunday programme was introduced on 28th March 1934 most of the usual Tilling changes were included; the 147 between Shoreditch and Knockholt Pound was re-introduced, and the 47B was withdrawn and replaced by extra buses on the 47 to Farnborough. Eighteen former Tilling STs from Bromley were joined by ten LTs from Dalston (D). The 146B to Downe was worked by four buses from Bromley, whilst Elmers End took over the 146 and 146A. Six extra buses were added to the 136 from TB making a total of twenty-six, due to a frequency increase to every eight minutes. One extension that did not take place was the 1 on Sundays to Chislehurst and Green Street Green, which was replaced by an extension of 610 to work Lewisham and Green Street Green, operated by Sidcup. Opportunity was taken to dispense with the long garage journeys from Croydon on the 49C and from Catford on the 159C, Streatham taking over the Sunday work on both of these services. Alternatively 11 more Catford buses were put on to the 21A. Eleven Croydon STs were put on Sunday route 144 (Streatham and Friern Barnet), joining 11 LTs from Muswell Hill. As the route was at the same time withdrawn between South Croydon and Streatham, long garage journeys from Croydon were still needed but these ceased on 30th September.

Commencing 16th May 1934, route 254 was diverted in Croham Road via Park Hill Road and sent on to West Croydon Station, thus avoiding the low bridge that had necessitated the use of open-top STLs. The frequency was improved to every 7½ minutes on weekdays, when six STs were required. Although Tilling type STs were used on this, the following ex-General STs were transferred to Croydon on 11th April: STs 33, 70/9, 86/8, 93, 433, and 703. Over at Bromley on Saturdays from 19th May, four ex-Tilling STs were worked on route 411

ST 1010 was one of four Bromley buses which ran on Saturdays on the 411 between Sidcup and Bromley. This particular working ran only from May to October 1934 and the route was then re-numbered 51.

(Sidcup Station and Bromley North). It was a former East Surrey service taken over by LGOC in 1932 and worked from Sidcup. The Bromley duties were taken off on 3rd October, when the route was renumbered 51.

Having gained the monopoly of London bus routes, the LPTB were able to introduce a renumbering scheme on 3rd October 1934, thereby dispensing with the restrictions of the Bassom system. Suffix letters were no longer employed for short workings, but instead were applied to diversions from the main route. Single-deck routes were renumbered into a separate 200 series.

Allocations at the former Tilling garages as at 3rd October 1934 are shown below:

New No.	Formerly	Route details
1	1C	Willesden – Lewisham
12	12A/E	South Croydon – Shepherds Bush
12	112/A/C	East Dulwich – Harlesden
21	21/A/B	Wood Green – Farningham
21A	20D	Wood Green – Old Kent Road
36	36	West Kilburn – Hither Green
47	47/A/B	Shoreditch – Farnborough
59	58/E	Camden Town – Chipstead Valley Road
59	59A/B	Camden Town – Coulsdon
64	254	West Croydon – Selsdon
75	75	Woolwich – Caterham Valley
78	78/A	Shoreditch – West Wickham
89	289/A/E	Plumstead Common – Bromley Common (early journey to Westerham Hill)
136	136	West Kilburn – Southborough
137	536/C	Highgate – West Wickham
146	146/A	Lewisham – Westerham Hill
146A	146B	Lewisham – Downe
159	159/A/C	Camden Town – South Croydon
194	179	West Wickham – Croydon Aerodrome
227	109/A/B	Penge – Welling

Garage	Type	Mon-Fri	Sat	Sun
TL	ST	19	19	16
TL	ST	7	7	39
TC	ST	15	17	0
ED	STL	11	9	0
TL	ST	16	14	14
ED	STL	6	0	0
AH	LT	18	15	0
S	LT	17	17	14
TL	ST	15	24	12
SP	ST	24	21	15
WG	ST	0	0	8
TL	ST	5	0	0
WG	ST	5	0	0
TB	STL	36	36	20
TL	STL	9	9	11
TB	ST	18	16	24
TL	ST	3	3	0
D	LT	9	10	8
TC	STL	10	0	13
TC	ST	5	8	0
AK	LT	9	10	10
TC	STL	21	24	17
TC	ST	11	10	7
TC	ST	6	4	3
TL	ST	14	16	18
TC	ST	14	18	12
TL	ST	24	23	0
AH	ST	10	11	12
ED	STL	0	0	13
TB	ST	14	15	0
TB	ST	18	16	26
TL	ST	7	7	7
CF	STL	3	3	6
TL	ST	7	8	6
TC	ST	10	10	15
P	ST	11	8	0
AK	LT	0	7	0
TC	ST	0a	0	0
ED	NS	14	14	8
TB	T	11	12	12
ED	LT*	4	8	8

*Single-deck   a Plus 4 ex route 12

As the 179 service ran the same way as 194 (Croydon-West Wickham) it became a section of that route and the four ex-Tilling STs continued the peak hour duties under the number 194 until they were withdrawn on 29th April 1936, the ED allocation then being increased and the route extended to Forest Hill. From the same date the allocation of the 12, South Croydon to Oxford Circus section was changed, the TC quota reduced to ten and the ED increased to 17.

On 17th April 1935, route 136 was withdrawn between Grove Park and Southborough and route 49 taken off between Lewisham and Crystal Palace. In replacement a new daily route 94 was introduced between Crystal Palace and Southborough via Forest Hill, Brockley and Lewisham. Bromley provided five STs on weekdays and nine on Sundays with Streatham operating 13 STs weekdays and nine on Sundays. The 136 continued to work from Bromley garage but reduced to 15 STs. The summer Sunday programme introduced 19th April included the Shoreditch-Knockholt Pound service, this time under the number 47. From 5th June a Saturday and Sunday extension of the 47 to Green Street Green commenced, being withdrawn from 2nd October.

Two new single-deck routes commenced working in

the Croydon area in 1935. The first on 5th June was the 235 running between South Croydon (Swan and Sugar Loaf) and Selsdon (Farley Road) via Croham Valley Road. This route was identical to the original 254 service. It ran weekdays only every 15 minutes, ten minutes in peak hours and Saturdays. It needed three buses and as no suitable single deckers were available, four elderly S type (Ss 369/71, 873/87) were brought out of store and relicensed and allocated to Croydon garage. Although unpopular with the public, they continued in use until 16th March 1936 when they were replaced by Ts 28, 34 and 39. Eventually in early 1939 LT single deckers took over this route. The other new Croydon route was introduced on 11th September 1935. Numbered 203, it worked daily between Purley (Old Lodge Lane) and Riddlesdown (Mitchley Avenue) every 20 or 30 minutes and was operated by two one-man buses. Once more London Transport had no spare vehicles of this kind so three 20-seater Gilford coaches, MT 1800, ABH 366 and UR 2402 were taken out of store, transferred to the Central Bus Division for Croydon garage, repainted red and numbered GF 193-195. During April and May 1936 these Gilfords were withdrawn and replaced by three Dennis Darts, DA 4, 19 and 41.

A number of former Independent buses acquired by London Transport were transferred to Croydon garage in 1935. First were the five Pickup STLs, which since their withdrawal from the 254 route had been fitted with covered-top decks. STL 554 came back to Croydon in February 1935, STLs 553/5/6 in April and STL 557 in July. STLs 555/7 went to Elmers End in April 1936 and in November that year finished up at Catford garage. In August 1935 Croydon had four more ex-independent buses. These were AEC Regents GJ 8501 ex-Chariot, VX 7487 ex-Empire, VX 7553 ex-Pro Bono Publico and GJ 3020 ex-Pembroke. They were given numbers ST 1028 to ST1031 and with their open staircases and old-fashioned board indicators they fitted in well with the Tilling STs with which they worked, mostly on the 75

route but sometimes on the 59. These additional STs and STLs replaced the LGOC ST type at Croydon. In September 1935, about 22 petrol engined STLs numbered between 503 and 584 were transferred to Catford from Hackney (H). Some earlier STLs in the 400s were in the Catford fleet by 1936 and possibly these were also replacements for many of the ex-LGOC STs. Another former independent bus with outside staircase, STL 558 ex-Redline (GW 2294), worked from Catford and Croydon from 1936.

A short extension of the 64 route took place on 4th March 1936 from Selsdon to Addington (Featherbed Lane). The Sunday extension of the 137 beyond Elmers End to West Wickham was withdrawn on 8th April 1936. On the same day route 78 was extended on Sundays from West Wickham to Croydon Airport, being operated by Nunhead and Elmers End garages. Catford had ceased to provide any Sunday working on 78 since 28th March 1934. A number of changes in the allocations of former Tilling routes took place on 29th April 1936. The 20 STLs working out of Catford on the 21 service were taken off, being replaced by increased allocations from Sidcup and West Green (WG). Instead, Catford took over the operation of route 54 (Plumstead Common and Selsdon). Twenty-one STLs were in use on this route, which conveniently passed outside the garage. The weekday working on the 78 was changed as it was withdrawn between West Wickham and Lower Sydenham and replaced by an extension of the 194 from West Wickham to Forest Hill. The 78 then operated between Shoreditch and Dulwich every four minutes and every eight minutes to Lower Sydenham, worked by 18 STs from Catford and ten LTs from Nunhead. Also on 29th April there were changes at Croydon with the 59 route, which due to traffic congestion in central London was operated in three sections, Camden Town and Coulsdon, Thornton Heath and Chipstead Valley and Camden Town and Croydon Airport. The latter being a diversion at Thornton Heath Pond along Purley

In 1935 four AEC Regents acquired from Independent operators were transferred to Croydon garage. ST 1028, formerly owned by Chariot, is seen on the way to Woolwich on route 75. With its open staircase body, it fitted in well with the former Tilling STs.

Way, it was numbered 59A and ran on weekdays only. Each section ran every ten or 12 minutes on weekdays. A through service was maintained on Sundays between Camden Town and Coulsdon every five minutes and at ten minute intervals on to Chipstead Valley. Croydon worked the 59A with 15 STs Monday to Friday and 18 on Saturdays. Route 59 lost five STLs from Croydon, but Streatham (AK) gained nine more LTs. Croydon gave up working on the 159 on weekdays but retained the 15 buses on Sundays.

During March and April 1936 the entire allocation of AEC Regals, the Tilling T type, was transferred from Bromley to Kingston (K) and replaced by six-wheeled single-deck LTs with their larger capacity. LTs 1050/3/5/ 8/60/1/82/90, 1141/54/78/92 were transferred to Bromley, mainly from Dalston (D) where Q types were taking over. The 227 had become a busy route with a frequent service, but it was not possible to use double deckers because of low bridges, including the one at Shortlands, and the Chislehurst Arch, which straddled the road.

A survey taken in May and June 1936 showed that Bromley routes were all operated by former Tilling ST or STL double deckers. At Croydon also, all the double-deck routes were mainly using former Tilling buses assisted by the ex-independent vehicles. Catford, however, had more of a mixed fleet. Although long-standing routes still largely used former Tilling buses, the later LPTB-type STLs were operated on the 54 and 137 services.

With the introduction of the winter programme on 7th October 1936, the usual withdrawal of the summer Sunday routes took place; that of the 47 south of Farnborough and the 146 to Westerham Hill. It was with the daily routes in the Catford and Bromley area that some rearrangement took place. The 89 (Plumstead Common and Bromley Common) was withdrawn and the 137 was withdrawn between Catford, Beckenham Hill Road and Elmers End and extended on Monday to

Saturday to Bromley (Chatterton Arms). The early morning journey to Westerham Hill was also taken over by the 137. A new route 154 was introduced on weekdays working jointly with the 54 between Plumstead Common and Elmers End, but this made a diversion at Blackheath by way of Marlborough Lane and Shooters Hill Road. Both the 54 and 154 ran every ten minutes, thus covering for the absence of the 89. A similar number of buses were in use though re-distributed. The revised 137 had the same number of STLs out of Catford. The former Bromley STs off the 89 enabled Bromley to take over the eight duties on the 146A from Catford and to add an additional five buses to the 47 replacing six Catford buses. Thus TL garage was able to put 14 buses on to the 154. On Sundays the 137 ran only to Catford garage with 15 STLs from Catford and 18 STLs from Chalk Farm (CF). This changed with the summer programme introduced on the 28th March 1937, when the 137 was projected to Bromley on Sunday afternoons and a Bromley allocation was added from Sunday 16th May. A Sunday service was also operated on the 154 between Lewisham and Selsdon, running with the 54 to Addiscombe thence via Cherry Orchard Road to Croydon. This had commenced on 28th March and Elmers End and Catford each provided seven buses.

The building of a new estate at Hayes led to the introduction on 4th August of a new single-deck route 232 between Beckenham Junction and Coney Hall. It was worked by three T type from Catford garage, namely T 37, 41 and 44, joined later by T 31. On 8th September the 137 left Tilling territory entirely when it was withdrawn between Hyde Park Corner and Bromley Common and diverted to Clapham Common. It was covered by the 36 and 136 routes up to New Cross but the Brockley to Stanstead Road section was left to the 74 tram route. Route 89 was revived, this time running from Welling (Guy Earl of Warwick) to its previous terminal at Bromley Common. It had replaced the 21A service between Lewisham, Shooters Hill and Welling,

A rear view of an ex-Tilling STL on the 89 service taken at Bromley South. This picture shows how the back of the bus has changed since Tilling days (compare with STL 105 on page 69), though the Aspro advertisement has been retained.

The former Tilling Regal T 315 is seen at Beckenham after the route number had been changed from 109 to 227. The large Tilling blind box has been reduced to take the standard size LPTB blind. Below The former open-topped Pickup STLs had been fitted with top covers in 1935 and they then looked not unlike the early LPTB STLs with similar blind displays. STL 555 is seen at the Forest Hill terminus of the 124.

and it once more took over the early morning journey to Westerham Hill. Bromley provided 14 STs on Monday to Friday and 18 at weekends. The 94 was also reallocated on weekdays to Catford with 18 STLs instead of five from Bromley and 13 from Streatham. From 27th March 1938 Catford acquired the full Sunday working as well. Another change took place with the 78 from 8th September as it was withdrawn between Lower Sydenham and East Dulwich (Grove Hotel) on weekdays; 23 Catford STs provided the Monday to Friday service and 12 Catford and 11 Nunhead LTs on Saturdays. Included in the seasonal Sunday withdrawals on 10th October was the 154, which was withdrawn from Selsdon and diverted to Croydon garage; this was taken off entirely on Sundays a year later.

Another reorganisation took place in the Croydon area on 5th January 1938 and route 59 was revised to work on weekdays between Thornton Heath and Chipstead Valley Road every six minutes. Additional peak hour journeys ran on Mondays to Fridays between Camden Town and Croydon garage. Route 59A was on weekdays withdrawn between Thornton Heath and Croydon Airport and diverted to Addiscombe (Black Horse). Route 115 (Wallington and Streatham Common) was extended via Norbury to Croydon Airport in replacement for the 59A, its allocation becoming five STLs from Sutton (A) and seven STs from Croydon. The Croydon allocation on the 59 was reduced from 43 STLs to 25 STs, and merely 13 STLs on Saturdays, whilst the allocation for the through journeys on Sundays remained 25 STLs from TC and 15 LTs from AK. The 59A was entirely a Streatham operation but Croydon helped out on Saturdays with 17 STs. To make up for the lost work at TC garage, 29 STLs were put on to route 133 (Liverpool Street and South Croydon) together with ten STLs from Merton (AL) and six LTs from AK. Also on 5th January, the 146A was withdrawn between Lewisham and Bromley North on Mondays to Fridays.

Catford garage gained two new routes on 4th May 1938. The first was the 124 working between Eltham (Southend Crescent), Grove Park and Forest Hill, which was in fact the renumbering and double decking of route 209, previously a Sidcup operation. It needed seven STLs from TL on weekdays, rising to 11 on Saturdays and nine on Sundays. The second new route was the 160 from Catford (St Dunstans College) to Welling, serving the Middle Park Estate, which used eight STs from TL Monday to Friday, 11 on Saturday, and nine STLs on Sunday. Route 227 was withdrawn between Chislehurst

Left **The 119 was a new route between Bromley and Croydon which commenced on 9th August 1939 and was worked by ex-Tilling buses from Bromley garage. ST 984 was photographed later that month.** Right **Rear view of ST 950, which is standing at Addiscombe (Black Horse) in 1939, whilst working on the short section of route 12 between Croydon Katharine Street and Addiscombe. None of the places shown on the route board would have applied on this journey.**

and Welling, being replaced between Chislehurst and Eltham by new route 161 operated by Sidcup and between Eltham and Welling by the new Catford route 160. The entire allocation of the 227 was transferred to Elmers End together with the single-deck LT buses, being a break from the familiar operation from Bromley in Tilling days and after.

On 3rd August 1938, route 203 was withdrawn and replaced by an extension of the 234 beyond Purley to Riddlesdown, and new route 234A which operated between Carshalton, Wallington and Purley (Old Lodge Lane). Neither were worked by Croydon at the time. On the same day, single-deck route 232 was withdrawn from Beckenham Junction and diverted to Bromley North, the Catford allocation of three T type being transferred to Bromley garage. Further operation on route 51 was provided by Bromley with six STLs on Mondays to Fridays and nine on Saturdays, whilst Croydon acquired six Sunday duties on route 197 (Croydon and Norwood Junction).

Commencing 12th October 1938, an extra service was added to the 12 route between Croydon and Addiscombe (Black Horse) operated by five STs from Croydon garage on Monday/Friday and four on Saturdays. It replaced the 178 service that had previously operated between these points over the same roads as the 12 with buses from Elmers End garage.

There were only four major route alterations in the former Tilling area during 1939, starting on 4th January with route 59. Alternate buses on the Thornton Heath to Chipstead Valley route were diverted at Coulsdon to serve a growing estate at Old Coulsdon by a circular route via Stoat's Nest Road and Marlpit Lane. This was numbered 59B and ran weekdays only. When the summer weekend changes commenced on 6th May, the 146A was extended on Saturdays and Sundays from Bromley to Lewisham and the increased Sunday working needed six buses from Catford as well as seven from Bromley. Instead of the 146, route 89 was extended every 30 minutes on Saturday afternoons and Sundays to Westerham Hill. Lastly, two new routes started from Croydon. The first, on the 5th July, was numbered 130 and ran daily from Croydon (Barclay Road) to New Addington every 30 minutes, operated by two STs. The other was the 119, which commenced 9th August and also ran daily, from Croydon (Barclay Road) to Bromley North via West Wickham and Hayes, five ex-Tilling STs from Bromley providing a 20-minute frequency. It is interesting that the last new pre-war route should connect the two Tilling centres of Croydon and Bromley.

The following summary shows the operation of the former Tilling area routes on 7th June 1939, and upon comparing this with the summary on 3rd October 1934 it will be seen how many allocations are very similar.

Number	Route
1	Willesden – Lewisham
12	South Croydon – Shepherds Bush
12	Croydon – Addiscombe
12	East Dulwich – Harlesden
21	Wood Green – Farningham
36	West Kilburn – Hither Green
47	Shoreditch – Knockholt Pound
51	Sidcup – Bromley North Station
54	Plumstead Common – Selsdon
59	Camden Town – Croydon Garage
	Thornton Heath – Chipstead Valley Road
59B	Thornton Heath – Old Coulsdon
59	Camden Town – Chipstead Valley (Suns)
59A	Camden Town – Addiscombe
64	West Croydon – Addington
75	Caterham Valley – Woolwich
78	Shoreditch – East Dulwich
	Shoreditch – Croydon Airport (Sundays)
89	Welling – Westerham Hill
94	Crystal Palace – Southborough
115	Wallington – Croydon Airport
124	Forest Hill – Eltham
133	Liverpool Street – South Croydon
136	West Kilburn – Grove Park
146A	Lewisham – Downe
154	Plumstead Common – Elmers End
159	Camden Town – South Croydon
160	Catford – Welling
197	Croydon – Norwood Junction
232	Bromley North – Hayes, Coney Hall
235	South Croydon – Selsdon

Garage	Type	Mon-Fri	Sat	Sun
TL	ST	19	19	11
X	ST	0	0	11
TL	ST	8	0	30
TC	ST	10	6	0
ED	LT	17	17	0
AH	LT	0	11	10
TC	ST	5	4	0
TL	ST	17	23	0
ED	LT	6	9	0
AH	LT	18	6	19
S	LT	17	17	14
TL	STL	0	0	15
SP	LT	43	44	15
WG	ST	0	0	13
TB	STL	28	25	22
TL	STL	17	20	10
TB	ST	23	19	19
D	STL	10	12	16
TB	STL	6	9	0
SP	LT	0	0	7
TL	STL	21	21	10
ED	LT	0	0	18
TC	ST	25	0	0
TC	STL	0	15	0
TC	STL	0	0	25
TC	ST	0	0	15
TC	ST	0	17	0
AK	LT	20	17	0
TC	ST	8	6	4
TC	ST	14	18	15
TL	ST	14	16	15
TL	ST	23	12	0
AH	LT	0	11	9
ED	LT	0	0	23
TB	STL	14	20	16
TL	STL	18	22	18
TC	ST	5	5	0
A	STL	5	5	5
TL	STL	7	11	9
TC	STL	29	16	0
AK	LT	6	29	0
AL	STL	10	0	0
TB	ST	15	15	9
Q	STL	0	0	8
TB	STL	5	8	7
TL	STL	0	0	6
TL	STL	14	0	0
TL	ST	0	14	0
TC	STL	0	0	15
AK	ST	39	18	0
Q	STL	0	17	0
TL	ST	8	11	9
TC	STL	0	0	6
ED	LT	9	12	0
TB	T(s/d)	3	3	4
TC	LT(s/d)	3	3	0

In the above summary, the STs shown at TB, TC and TL were all the ex-Tilling type plus a handful of former Independent vehicles. During 1938, the remaining Tilling STLs at Catford were transferred to Bromley, while Catford had instead a number of the later LPTB style STL with petrol engines. Since 1934 all the new London Transport buses had been powered by diesel engines and in March 1939 a start was made in converting a number of the petrol-engined STLs to diesel power, and so many of those allocated to Catford were withdrawn for this purpose and replaced by other buses, mainly in the STL 200-300 series.

The outbreak of war in September 1939 put an end to much of the Tilling heritage, causing reduction in services, the reallocation of vehicles away from former Tilling garages or the taking over of other routes. Many of the former Tilling vehicles themselves were subject to premature withdrawal or operation on other duties.

9 The Second World War and After 1939-1949

When the Prime Minister, Neville Chamberlain, made the announcement at 11am on Sunday 3rd September 1939 that Britain was at war with Germany it came at the end of over 12 months of fear and tension, much of the population having realised that war was inevitable. Preparations had been made in many respects; air raid shelters were being built in public parks, and a general distribution of gas masks had been made. London Transport had been working on contingency plans for some time.

The Government soon imposed drastic fuel restrictions, particularly in respect of petrol, so it was fortunate that so many buses were then fitted with oil engines. The LPTB were obliged to reduce their operations and so withdrew many vehicles from service, particularly those running on petrol. These withdrawals included most of the ST class, with their limited capacity, and the ex-Tilling buses with the non-standard bodies. The first batch was taken out of service and stored at the end of September 1939, the second in the middle of October and the last on 1st November. Included in these were the Tilling STs from the three garages, Catford, Bromley and Croydon. The scheduled fleet on 18th October showed that Catford had diesel-engined STLs whilst Bromley and Croydon had STLs with petrol engines, Catford's Tilling type STLs having been sent to Bromley.

The fuel restrictions and the reduced fleet meant a reduction in bus services and many routes were withdrawn, curtailed or had a reduced frequency; thus routes were taken off where they were covered by other services. At Catford, the 154 route was withdrawn entirely on 23rd September 1939 as it was sufficiently covered by the 54. Long garage journeys were avoided where possible and this affected many routes working from former Tilling garages. On 18th October route 12 was extended from Park Royal to Harlesden on weekdays (previously only a few journeys) due to the withdrawal of route 18A. In order to conserve fuel, Catford's 25 duties on the two sections of the 12 route were taken off and replaced by an increased number of LTs from Nunhead. It is therefore a little surprising that Catford returned to the route on 15th May 1940 and that the consequent garage journeys continued for the rest of the war years. The long garage journeys from Bromley on the 36 route also ceased on 18th October following a revision of the timetable, under which the route worked in two sections, West Kilburn and Peckham High Street (with 15 buses from Camberwell) and West Kilburn and Hither Green (with 26 buses from Catford). TL's share on route 1 was reduced to ten buses on weekdays but increased again later. The remaining Sunday duties on route 21 also disappeared, although a few Catford buses reappeared at times during 1940.

Further changes took place on 22nd November 1939. Route 89 was withdrawn between Lewisham and Bromley Common and reallocated to Catford with 12 STLs. The 146A ran as a daily service between Bromley North and Downe only. The early journey to Westerham Hill previously worked from the 89 was operated from Bromley North under the number 146. The 136 service was withdrawn between Grove Park and Victoria, its remaining section diverted to Victoria Coach Station and reallocated to Middle Row (X) garage. The Lewisham to Grove Park section of the 136 was covered by the 94. The 94 also was changed, Bromley garage joining Catford in working the route with 12 buses from each. Following the loss of the 89 route, the 47 was left to cover the roads to Bromley and the Sunday extension to Knockholt Pound was lost. The operation of route 51 was taken over entirely by Bromley, the route being

STL 111 has been altered to comply with blackout regulations with reduced lighting and white mudguards for better visibility at night. It is a Croydon bus on route 64.

withdrawn on weekdays between Farnborough and Bromley North, but continuing to Bromley on Sundays. There were changes at Croydon on 22nd November when the remaining Monday to Friday peak hour journeys on the 59 and 59B were withdrawn between Thornton Heath Pond and Camden Town. In common with many London bus routes the evening service was reduced or curtailed. The revised allocation meant just 14 STLs from Croydon on the 59 and 59B on weekdays, with Croydon and Streatham providing ten STLs each for the extended 59 on Sundays. Fifteen STLs from Croydon replaced Streatham's buses on the 59A. Streatham took over full operation of the 159 on Sundays, but from 3rd January 1940 TC provided 13 STLs on Monday to Friday and five on Saturday until 19th April 1944 when, following other variations, TC settled down to a Sunday-only operation on the route. Other changes included a reduction from 29 to 16 of the Croydon buses on 133, AK taking over the majority of the allocation. Fourteen TC buses were put on the 68 (Chalk Farm and South Croydon) on Sundays but this lasted only until 20th November 1940. This was the first time that Croydon based buses had worked on this long route.

A number of other changes took place a week later on 29th November. Route 75 was withdrawn between West Croydon and Caterham Valley, the 197 instead being extended from Croydon to Caterham. Croydon garage withdrew from the 75, leaving Catford to provide 21 STLs daily. Croydon then took over the entire operation of the extended 197 with 16 STLs. Croydon also acquired 12 of the Sunday duties on the 54 and later, on 4th December 1940, provided eight Monday to Friday duties for the remainder of the war. Route 78 was withdrawn on Sundays between Dulwich and Croydon Airport and on weekdays at East Dulwich between the Grove Hotel and The Plough. It therefore ran daily from Dulwich to Shoreditch. The Catford buses with their long garage run were taken off, being replaced by nine LTs from Nunhead and eight STLs from Dalston. The long association of routes 21 and 78 with Catford garage had therefore ceased, the Sunday operation of the 21 from TL having ended earlier in 1940. A further break with Tilling tradition occurred on 22nd April 1942 when the 21 route was withdrawn between Moorgate and Turnpike Lane.

With the approach of winter in 1940 the authorities were concerned with what might happen to the commuter traffic during the dark mornings and evenings, especially if rail and tram transport were badly affected by bombing. Therefore, a number of Monday to Friday peak hour express sections were introduced on certain routes during November and December 1940. These included limited stop journeys on route 47 between Bromley Market Place and London Bridge using STs or STLs from TB garage. Route 133 had an express section worked by Croydon garage between Streatham Station and London Bridge. The Express services were not a success and all were withdrawn from 19th March 1941.

By the summer of 1940 the war had taken a turn for the worse, with frequent air raids on London. Many buses had been destroyed or damaged and this led to many of the stored ST type buses being put back into service. However, six of the Tilling STs were sold, four to the BBC in May 1940, one to Ministry of Supply in July and two months later another to HM Dockyard, Devonport. In September 1940 eight STs were relicensed for service, seven of them returning to Croydon garage

and taking up duties again on such routes as 12 or 59. Many of the withdrawn buses, including Tilling STs, were in store at Bull Yard in Peckham, the former Tilling overhaul works. On the night of 23rd October 1940 these premises were completely burnt out as a result of enemy action and 48 vehicles were destroyed, including Tilling STs 890, 927/38/65/7/73/4/80/90/1/2, 1003/7/8/10/21 and the bodies of STs 853/76, 954/97. Two former Independent buses, ST 1030/1, were also included in the total.

During November 1940 ninety-three former Tilling STs were relicensed, being sent to many different garages in London. Nine were allocated to Catford garage and nine to Bromley, and these were soon in use on familiar routes, but the others ran on various routes throughout London and the small Tilling type blind box meant that only the ultimate destination and route number could be shown. From 35 more licensed in December 1940, twenty-seven went to Country area garages. Lastly, 12 more entered service in January and February 1941, resulting in a total of 149 Tilling STs back in operation. But not for long; a few were withdrawn in August 1941 and the remainder were back in store by October 1941. Although the majority of the Tilling STs had been found suitable for further service, in December 1940 twenty (including the four damaged at Bull Yard) became rest rooms for the Home Guard and these were ultimately scrapped.

In October 1940 London Transport issued an appeal to provincial operators for buses. A total of 475 were sent on loan to London from 51 operators and were distributed to various garages in London including some in the Country area. Most of them arrived before the end of October and two North Western Dennis Lancets, JA 2298/2300, and a Eastern Counties Tilling-Stevens B10A, DX 8587, were sent to Catford, moving to ED within two weeks. Two West Yorkshire Lancets, YG 5712/3, spent a few days at Bromley, but it was Croydon which retained most of the provincial buses longest. Between 29th October and 7th November ten buses on loan were sent to TC garage, being Newcastle Regent VK 2380, Hull Regent RH 4776, Dundee Leyland TD1 TS 9117, Eastern National Leyland Lion VW 4578, Plymouth Dennis Lance DR 9062, two Tilling-Stevens buses, Benfleet UN 2681 and Portsmouth RV 1137, and three Manchester Corporation Crossley Condors, VU 3635, VR 6013/6683. The first seven went to other garages on 2nd December and Croydon received five more Manchester Condors, VR 7536, VU 774/83, 3644/58. These were operated on routes 12 and 133. Alas, two of the buses, VR 6013 and VU 3658, were destroyed in the Croydon garage fire, the others going back to Manchester on 3rd August 1941.

It was on one of the worst nights of the London 'Blitz', 10th May 1941, that Croydon garage was burnt out as the result of incendiary bombs. Fifty-six buses were destroyed including two Tilling STs, ST 893/5, and 20 Tilling STLs, STL 53, 71, 82/7/8/96-101/4/7/10/2/6/20/7/9/30. Two others (STLs 80/4) lost their bodies but the chassis were in good enough condition to be fitted with float Tilling bodies. Among the other buses destroyed was ex-Pickup STL 554. Buses came from many garages to make up the losses, and although the next day vehicles were operating without windows or with scorch marks, it was claimed that the morning service was near normal. Later in the war, Elmers End garage, which was also used as an overhaul shop, was hit by a 'doodlebug' on 18th July 1944 and STL 63 and ST 879 were destroyed.

ST 953 was one of the buses relicensed for further service and was allocated to Bromley garage, so it was possible for it to use its normal route and destination details for route 47. It was seen at Farnborough terminus on Sunday 21st September 1941 standing alongside a Dalston STL. In order to keep buses running, damaged windows were simply boarded over.

STL 94 is working on the Bromley to Croydon route 119 and has been fitted with anti-blast netting at most windows as a protection for passengers in the event of an air raid. This was a feature on most buses in the Second World War years.

In the latter part of the War many of the Tilling and indeed General STs were loaned to provincial operators. ST 983 was on loan to *City of Oxford* for nearly five years. Here it stands next to a new utility lowbridge bus.

By December 1941 it was the turn of provincial operators to have help from London Transport and many ST buses including 147 Tilling type were sent away on loan. Some buses were loaned to two or three different undertakings, and altogether 47 operators used London buses. Most returned to London late in 1944 or early 1945, but a few stayed away longer, for example Crosville and City of Oxford retained buses until 1946 and Hants & Dorset kept two ex-Tillings until February 1948.

Not many route changes took place in the former Tilling area during the war years but the following should be mentioned. On 24th March 1940 route 159 was extended to Chipstead Valley on Sundays. The summer Sunday extension of route 47 to Knockholt

Pound ran for the first two war years, first from 24th March 1940 until November and again on 6th April 1941 until 26th October 1941. During 1940, the 47 had been extended to Green Street Green on Saturdays from 15th May and on Mondays to Fridays from 5th June, this extension being withdrawn on 13th November 1940. The weekday early morning journey to Green Street Green that had been working since 1932 was retained and continued until April 1943. But the similar early morning journey to Westerham Hill on 146 was withdrawn on 3rd July 1940 as there were restrictions on buses penetrating the Biggin Hill aerodrome area. On 27th November route 232 was double-decked and renumbered 138, three STLs from Bromley (TB) covering the route between Bromley North and Coney

In November 1940 the single-deck 232 service was converted to double-deck operation and renumbered 138, STLs from Bromley being used for this purpose. STL 56 is standing at the terminus in the midst of the Coney Hall estate.

Hall. On Sundays from 19th January 1941 Croydon replaced ED on route 194 with 12 STLs, but by 2nd April these duties had returned. On 27th August Croydon lost the duties on route 130 to ED, who used LT type daily. A separate section was added on weekdays to route 51 from 29th October 1941, three LTs from Sidcup running from Sidcup Station to Green Street Green. This was a replacement for part of the single-deck 241 route (Welling and Green Street Green) which was then withdrawn south of Sidcup Station. The 51 was revised again on 9th December 1942 when alternate buses ran either to Farnborough or to Green Street Green on weekdays, the latter being numbered 51A. This operation was covered by the allocation of five Bromley STLs plus a similar number of Sidcup vehicles. The single-deck 235 service was taken off on 13th May 1942, being covered by a slight increase on route 64. On 3rd April 1944 Bromley garage joined in the operation of route 61 (Eltham and Bromley garage) by adding two STLs to the six LTs from Sidcup, and by 12th September 1945 SP and TB were each providing four weekday buses to the route, increased to five apiece the following February. On 19th April 1944 the working of routes 234

and 234A was transferred to Croydon from Sutton (A) garage. The two routes operated jointly from Wallington to Purley, then 234 ran to Purley (Mitchley Avenue) and the 234A to Old Lodge Lane. These daily services required six LT type single deckers.

During the 12 months following the end of the war attempts were made to return bus operation to normal. The 47 operated to Knockholt Pound on Sundays for the summer season from 26th May 1946 and from the same date an 89A service was introduced on Sundays running every half hour from Welling (Guy Earl of Warwick) to Westerham Hill, with Catford providing 16 STLs for this and the 89. These seasonal services were withdrawn from 13th October and also on that day the 159 was withdrawn from Chipstead Valley and operated instead to Old Coulsdon, thus providing a Sunday service to this point for the first time. Commencing 22nd May 1946, Croydon put ten buses on to route 68 (Chalk Farm and South Croydon) on weekdays, resulting in some reduction in the Norwood allocation.

The following summary shows the operation of buses from the former Tilling garages commencing 22nd May 1946.

Route Details		Mon-Fri	Sat	Sun	Other garages
BROMLEY (TB)					
47	Shoreditch – Farnborough	25 STL	24 STL	30 STL	D daily
	(Sun) Knockholt Pound	17 ST	17 ST	8 ST	
51	Sidcup Station – Farnborough	5 STL	5 STL	4 STL	SP daily
51A	Sidcup Station – Green Street Green	a	a	0	a Buses ex
51B	Sidcup Station – Orpington Station	a	a	0	route 51
61	Eltham – Bromley Garage	5 STL	5 STL	0	SP daily
94	Crystal Palace – Southborough	12 STL	11 STL	12 STL	TL daily
119	Bromley North Station – Croydon	12 STL	13 STL	10 STL	
138	Bromley North Station – Coney Hall	5 STL	5 STL	3 STL	
146A	Bromley North Station – Downe	3 STL	3 STL	8 STL	
CATFORD (TL)					
1	Willesden – Lewisham	29 ST	23 ST	8 STL	
12	South Croydon – Oxford Circus	20 STL	0	0	S, ED, AH daily
	(Sun) Shepherds Bush				TC Mon-Sat
	East Dulwich – Harlesden				
36	West Kilburn – Hither Green	29 STL	24 STL	18 STL	Q daily
54	Plumstead Common – Selsdon	18 STL	26 STL	12 STL	TC daily
75	West Croydon – Woolwich	31 STL	31 STL	25 STL	
89	Welling – Lewisham	12 STL	12 STL	16 STL	
89A	Welling – Westerham Hill	0	0	a	a Buses ex route 89
94	Crystal Palace – Southborough	12 STL	17 STL	11 STL	TB daily
124	Forest Hill – Eltham	12 STL	15 STL	12 STL	
160	Catford – Welling	6 STL	8 STL	6 STL	
CROYDON (TC)					
12	South Croydon – Oxford Circus	11 ST	10 ST	0	also ED & TL
			14 STL		
54	Plumstead Common – Selsdon	12 ST	6 ST	10 ST	TL daily
59	Camden Town – Chipstead Valley (Sun)	0	0	10 STL	AK Suns
59	Thornton Heath – Chipstead Valley	16 ST	14 ST	0	
59B	Thornton Heath – Old Coulsdon	a	a	0	a Buses ex route 59
64	West Croydon – Selsdon or Addington	7 STL	7 STL	4 STL	
68	Chalk Farm – South Croydon	10 STL	5 STL	0	N, CF daily
115	Wallington – Croydon Airport	6 STL	7 STL	10 STL	A Mon-Sat
133	Liverpool Street Station – South Croydon	30 STL	20 STL	0	AK daily
159	Streatham – Old Coulsdon (Sun)	0	0	11 STL	
197	Caterham Valley – Norwood Junction	20 ST	17 ST	14 ST	
234	Wallington – Purley (Mitchley Avenue)	8 LT	8 LT	6 LT	Single-deck
234A	Wallington – Purley (Old Lodge Lane)	a	a	a	a Buses ex 234

The Tilling STL class was subject to various modifications at times owing to rebuilding, and STL 70 acquired an unusual four window arrangement on the front of the upper deck. It is seen when working on route 94.

After returning from the provinces, many Tilling STs were returned to service in London and used as spare buses at garages throughout the system. ST 882 is working from Leyton garage on a Sunday trip to High Beech.

The majority of Catford buses at that time were the standard diesel type and only two ex-Tilling buses remained amongst the batch of petrol engined STs, being ST 872/910 relicensed as spares. Although Croydon was beginning to acquire some diesel STLs a number of petrol engined STLs remained including the following 12 former Tilling buses, STL 52,65/6, 84, 103/9/11/3/8/24/6/8 plus one ST, ST 849. It is sad that so many had been lost in the fire during the war. Bromley's buses were still entirely petrol-engined and a number of former Tilling buses remained in service, these being STL 54-62/4/7-70/2-81/3/5/6/9-95, 102/8/14/5/7/9/21-3/5. Four of the former Pickup buses continued in use, STL 555/7 at Bromley and STL 553/6 at Croydon.

Gradually the position changed and eventually Croydon was allocated some new buses. These were some of the 65 standard post-war Leylands of the PD1 type included in the STD class. TC had the last nine of the buses delivered, which arrived between 11th and 23rd December 1946 and were numbered STD 163-5/8/71-4/6. They were used on route 115 as well as for relief work on the 133. Within a few months the STDs were transferred to Loughton (L) garage and Croydon became the second garage to receive some of the new RT3 type when in July 1947 RTs 154/5, 407 arrived followed by RTs 159, 410/1 in August and RTs 167/9/72 in September, replacing the STDs on the 115. Further RTs arrived in November and December 1947 and they replaced the older buses on the 133 and 197. In December 1947 and January 1948, Bromley also received an allocation of RT buses and Catford joined the ranks of RT users in June 1948. The number of new RT buses was not sufficient to cover the loss of obsolete vehicles, so in 1949 London Transport had on loan 180 new Bristol buses straight from the factory but painted in the livery of the provincial operators for whom they were intended. They ran in London for about a year and they were allocated to various garages in both Central and Country areas. Seven highbridge Eastern Counties buses in red livery were sent to Croydon and operated on route 68 from January 1949 to February 1950. They were HPW 95/8/9, 107/8/9/10. Catford also was allocated six lowbridge K5G Bristols, three Eastern Nationals, ONO 51/2/3 in May 1949 and three United Automobile Services, KHN 497/8/9. These lowbridge buses were used on the long 36 and 75 routes and were not popular in London. They went on to their respective owners in May 1950. To complete the loans, 21 older buses were borrowed from Leeds City Transport. These were AEC Regents with Roe bodies dating from 1934-1936, being ANW 671/4/6/9/93, AUM 409/11/14-16/9/21/9/32/7/57/9/60/3, CNW 902/4. They were on loan from September 1949 to June 1950 and all were allocated to Bromley garage and used mainly on routes 61 and 138.

Meanwhile certain changes in operation had taken place. Some rescheduling in November 1947 resulted in the Catford buses finally coming off route 12 and being replaced by an increased allocation from ED. So ended the long garage runs from Catford to Forest Hill and Dulwich, which had been in use since 1924. An important route change took place on 12th November 1947 when routes 59, 59A and 159 were withdrawn north of Oxford Circus and diverted to West Hampstead, whilst the northern terminus of the 53A from Plumstead Common was changed to Camden Town. From 7th April 1948 the weekday section of the 59 from Thornton Heath to Chipstead Valley was renumbered 166 and the 59B to Old Coulsdon as 166A.

An extreme shortage of buses in 1949 led London Transport to borrow a number of new Bristols from ex-Tilling BTC operators outside London. HPW 95 was one of seven highbridge K5G Bristols from Eastern Counties to be allocated to Croydon garage and usually operated on route 68. Both destinations and service number are shown on one blind, the other taken up with the London Transport fleetname.

Catford also was allocated some Bristols, although they were lowbridge vehicles like this K5G of United Automobile Services.

During the war single-deck route 254, Bromley and Beckenham via Park Langley, had been converted to double-deck and renumbered 126 but had always been operated by Elmers End. In one of the post-war readjustments most of the duties were transferred to Bromley as shown by this picture of STL 58.

In 1946 a number of Tilling STLs were transferred to the northern Country area, mainly for local or works services. Sometimes they were drawn into service on the trunk routes as seen in this example of STL 115 working on the 351 whilst allocated to Watford High Street garage.

STL 73, a bus in green livery, had been sent to the Country Area as a replacement but by July 1949 had returned to Bromley and resumed duties on local routes such as 138.

Left **ST 1027 was one of the Regents transferred to London from the Brighton fleet. It ended its days in the Special Events Fleet and in this instance is one of the large number of buses taking racegoers from Morden Station to Epsom Racecourse for the Derby in 1948. The body appears to be in an advance state of dilapidation** Right **STL 113 was another ex-Tilling transferred to the Special Events Fleet and the bus, with its badly bowed body, was put to work during its last year on a special Wimbledon Tennis Service.**

It is opportune to recall the later history of the former Tilling buses that survived the war. Only the STL class had remained in active service at the former Tilling garages, about 12 at Croydon and the rest at Bromley. In December 1946, following the delivery of the new STD buses, eight STLs (STLs 62/5/9, 90, 111/5/7/23) were transferred to the Country area garage at Hemel Hempstead, being operated on various works services. They were split up in February 1947, STLs 65 and 115 going to Watford High Street and STLs 62 and 111 to Leavesden Road. At the same time another bus, STL 128, joined them in the Country area at Leavesden Road. In January 1948, STL 73 replaced STL 90 which was

completely worn out. Six were eventually repainted green and they were all withdrawn during 1948 and 1949. Nine of the STLs in service were withdrawn in 1947, the others in 1948 and 1949, the last three — STLs 56, 83 and 118 — being withdrawn at Bromley in October 1949. STL 59 was fitted with a standard LPTB 56-seat body in December 1946 and STL 75 followed with a similar body in April 1947.

In March 1948 a Special Events Fleet was commenced using vehicles no longer considered as suitable for normal service, to be available for such duties as the Derby at Epsom or as Wimbledon Tennis Specials. Five buses included in this fleet in 1948 were STLs 91, 102/13/22/8, but these were withdrawn later that year. Four others were STLs 60 and 73 and the two that had been rebodied, STLs 59 and 75. These two lasted until this special fleet was disbanded in February 1950.

The 12 single-deck Regals, Ts 307-318, had been transferred to Kingston (K) garage in March/April 1936, where they stayed for a few years but moved about to many different garages subsequently. Ts 309/11/13/15/18 were dismantled early in 1949, and the others were sold later that year (except T 317 which was eventually sold in January 1953).

T 311, looking rather less resplendent than it does in the photograph on page 67, while working from Uxbridge garage. It moved to Hounslow for a brief spell before being withdrawn for scrapping in February 1949.

One of the last duties of the Tilling Regents was to serve as staff canteens based at certain garages around London. ST 867 (690J), along with ST 969 (689J), was put to use as a canteen at Cricklewood garage in December 1946.

It was the Tilling Regents, the ST class, that had the most varied existence. About 110 of those that had returned to London from their sojourn with the provincial operators were relicensed for further service with London Transport as spare buses and sent to garages throughout the system. In use they had little in the way of route description, sometimes merely the route number, and often paper stickers were used. From 1946, twenty-two were put to use as training buses. Most of these STs were withdrawn during 1947-1949, though some like ST 887 were in the Special Events Fleet. In fact, ST 887 was the last open staircase bus in use, being withdrawn in February 1950. Two of the STs were adapted as tree cutters in September 1945 and lasted until 1953; these were ST 865/70 (renumbered as 650/1 J in the service fleet). Six were put to use as staff canteens as follows: September 1946, ST 888 as 688J at WR garage: December 1946, ST 969 as 689J at W garage, also ST 867 as 690J at W; January 1947, ST 917 as 691J at K; March 1947, ST 951 as 692J at AK; and April 1947, ST 922 as 693J at AF. They were withdrawn March 1952, October 1951, May 1953, June 1952, October 1951 and November 1954 respectively.

Therefore ST 922 was the last Tilling bus to be withdrawn from service with London Transport.

We are indebted to the late Prince Marshall and the London Bus Preservation Group for the discovery and restoration of ST 922, which had been sold after being withdrawn as a canteen. This bus (registration number GJ 2098) had entered service late in 1930, numbered 6098 in the Tilling fleet and allocated to Catford garage where it first ran as TL 4 on route 12A (Oxford Circus and South Croydon) on weekdays and the 12E on Sundays from Shepherds Bush to Croydon. It stayed at Catford until withdrawal in 1941 and, after a spell with Midland Red during the war, became a staff canteen until sold in 1955. It has been extremely well restored in London Transport livery. Its frequent use in London in the 1970s, particularly on the Round London Tours and vintage bus route 100 enabled modern generations to experience a type of bus used in London for many years. Another enthusiast, Barry Weatherhead, has found a single-deck TS 7, XW 9892, which originally ran as TB 4 on route 109 from October 1925. After withdrawal it was sold for use by a showman and it is now hoped to restore this bus into full Tilling livery.

Thanks to the efforts of a number of enthusiasts led by the late Prince Marshall, ST 922 was extremely well restored and was to be seen in the 1970s on vintage bus routes and the Round London Sightseeing Tour. The bodywork was completely rebuilt by LPC Coachworks. These photographs show the bus in Buckingham Palace Road on the Sightseeing Tour and Westminster on one of the variations of route 100.

Although by the transfer of the London bus business to London Transport, Tilling had lost an important branch of their empire, they were able to concentrate on the many other concerns throughout the country in which they had a financial interest. It was in 1914 that Tilling first launched out in a bus operation away from London when 22 new single-deck Tilling-Stevens buses were built and sent down to Folkestone on the Kent coast. This was not operated under the name of Tilling but as Folkestone District Road Car Co Ltd, which was later to form part of the larger East Kent company in 1916. The approach to the Brighton area was different, as Tilling first obtained 12 licences to operate buses in Hove and sent a number of TTA1 buses there from the London fleet pending the delivery of new TS3 type buses. In 1916 Tilling bought out the Brighton, Hove and Preston United Omnibus Co and so was established Tilling's Brighton and Hove Omnibus Section, all buses being operated under the name of Thomas Tilling.

Another provincial operation commenced in June 1919 when Tilling provided 12 Tilling-Stevens TS3 buses for operation in the Ipswich area, at first under their own name but from September 1919 as Eastern Counties Road Car Company. Although Tilling obtained an interest and control of many other bus companies, including National Omnibus and Transport Company Ltd, it was only in London and Brighton that the Company operated under its own name.

The Brighton operation therefore differed from all the other Tilling concerns in following more closely the type of vehicle and operating methods of London. Between 1916 and 1927 a total of 103 Tilling-Stevens TS3 petrol-electric buses were built for the Brighton fleet and, although similar to those in London, there were certain differences in that they were limited to a 43-seat body instead of 48-seat. Also, they were later permitted glass windscreens for the driver and pneumatic tyres. Following the experiments with covered-top TS17A and AEC buses, the first 12 of the new AEC Regents ran in Brighton. Eventually 110 Regents to exactly the same design as those for the London fleet were built by 1932 for Brighton (five were later sent to London). In 1934, eight more AEC Regents were built for Brighton but these had 56-seat bodies built by Tilling similar to London STLs.

All buses carried small stencil plates on the sides, but

No. 532, LH 9446, was one of the first buses specially built for service in Brighton in 1916. The standard 34-seat TTA1 body was used on a TS3 petrol-electric chassis. Note the large shield as protection for the driver, not permitted on London buses.

No. 1113, PM 8547, was a TS3A bus that entered the Brighton fleet in July 1925 and by 1930 it had been fitted with pneumatic tyres and some protection for the driver in the form of a glass windscreen, refinements not achieved by London TS3As by the time they were withdrawn.

the letters did not denote garages but the route or group of routes. Buses were allocated to a route and also a duty and remained on that duty whenever in service.

Thomas Tilling continued to work in Brighton until 26th November 1935 when a new company, Brighton, Hove and District Omnibus Company, was set up wholly-owned by Thomas Tilling. It thus joined the other Tilling group companies which were eventually sold to the British Transport Commission in September 1948. Thomas Tilling then continued as a holding company for various businesses other than road transport.

Following the transfer of Tilling's various bus companies to the British Transport Commission, a new company was formed under the name of Tillings Transport (BTC) Ltd in order to continue Tilling's coaching operations. These had commenced in 1906 when two Milnes-Daimlers had been fitted with saloon bodies for private hire work. By 1925 there were about six Tilling-Stevens TS3 coaches including at least four with IT registrations, IT 286, 407/10/1. Another six TS3s were acquired from Pickfords Ltd, these being IT 246-251. These coaches were garaged at Acorn Street, Camberwell. They were replaced in 1926 by 22 Tilling-

Stevens coaches of the later B9A class, which gave way in 1931 to 18 AEC Regals with Tilling built 30-seat coach bodies. At this time Tilling was supplying six coaches on contract to Imperial Airways, running between London and Croydon, and the contract continued almost to the end of the 1939/45 war. Subsequently a number of coaches of various makes were purchased and operated from Searles Road, New Kent Road, SE1, and 14 coaches remained to be transferred to the new Company in 1948. In June 1951 the business of Patrick Hearn was acquired by the BTC, comprising a fleet of 38 coaches and garage premises at Northdown Street, Kings Cross. The two fleets were merged and operated from Kings Cross under the name of Tillings Transport. By 1958 there were 43 coaches operated bearing the fleetname of 'Tilling'. Administration control and vehicle overhaul had been in the hands of Eastern National at Chelmsford since 1948 and by 1966 the vehicles were numbered into Eastern National's system. Eventually in 1974 the Company was absorbed into the new National Travel (South East) Ltd. Therefore after 70 years the name of Tilling disappeared from motor passenger transport in London.

A Tilling Regent on route 7, Portslade and Kemp Town. This bus, 6202, shows that the Brighton buses were almost identical to those operated in London, using the same style service number and destination blinds with the four-line route board underneath.

This side view of a Tilling Regent standing at Brighton station shows the one big difference with the London buses; the board carried below the upper deck windows showing extreme destinations, an item not seen on London buses since 1919.

Appendix A
Vehicles Owned or Operated by Thomas Tilling Ltd

1 Early fleet (1904–1912)
Column 1 gives the Tilling fleet number, column 2 the registration number, column 3 the chassis, whilst column 4 shows the date into service.

(1)	(2)	(3)	(4)		(1)	(2)	(3)	(4)
1	A 6934	Milnes Daimler 20hp	09/04		32	LC 3605	Straker Squire/Büssing	04/06
2	A 8215	Milnes Daimler 20hp	12/04		33	LC 3606	Straker Squire/Büssing	05/06
3	A 8216	Milnes Daimler 20hp	12/04		34	LC 3607	Straker Squire/Büssing	05/06
4	A 8649	Milnes Daimler 20hp	01/05		35	LC 3608	Straker Squire/Büssing	05/06
5	A 8540	Milnes Daimler 20hp	01/05		36	LC 3609	Straker Squire/Büssing	06/06
7	A 8657	Milnes Daimler 20hp	03/05		37	LC 3610	Straker Squire/Büssing	06/06
8	A 8658	Milnes Daimler 20hp	03/05		39	LC 3611	Milnes Daimler 28hp	07/06
6	A 8659	Milnes Daimler 20hp	04/05		40	LC 3612	Milnes Daimler 28hp	07/06
9	A 9730	Milnes Daimler 20hp	04/05		41	LC 3613	Milnes Daimler 28hp	07/06
—	?	Büssing (on trial)	05/05		43	LC 3614	Milnes Daimler 28hp	07/06
10	A 9969	Milnes Daimler 20hp	05/05		51	LC 3615	Milnes Daimler 28hp	12/06
14	LC 973	Milnes Daimler 20hp	07/05		53	LC 3616	Milnes Daimler 28hp	01/07
16	LC 1280	Milnes Daimler 20hp	07/05		55	LC 3617	Dennis	02/07
17	LC 2357	Milnes Daimler 20hp	09/05		61	LC 3618	Milnes Daimler 28hp	02/07
18	LC 2757	Milnes Daimler 20hp	10/05		63	LC 3619	Milnes Daimler 28hp	02/07
19	LC 2818	Milnes Daimler 20hp	10/05		68	LC 3620	Dennis	03/07
20	LC 3185	Milnes Daimler 28hp	12/05		?	LC 3621	Milnes Daimler 28hp	04/07
—	LC 3128	Dennis (on trial)	01/06		?	LC 3622	Milnes Daimler 28hp	04/07
22	LC 3600	Milnes Daimler 28hp	02/06		?	LC 3623	Dennis	04/07
25	LC 3601	Milnes Daimler 28hp	03/06		?	LC 3624	Dennis	04/07
27	LC 3602	Milnes Daimler 28hp	04/06		?	LC 3625	Dennis	06/07
28	LC 3603	Milnes Daimler 28hp	04/06		?	LC 3626	Dennis	06/07
30	LC 3504	Milnes Daimler 28hp	04/06		78	LC 3627	SB&S (Hallford)	01/08

Numbers 11, 12 and 13 were Royal Mail Vans, 15 (LC 2192) was a breakdown lorry, and LC 3621 and possibly 3622 were fitted with single-deck saloon bodies for Private Hire work. All the rest had 34-seat open-top double-deck bodies, the first three by Birch Bros of Kentish Town. It is probable that Tilling built all the other bodies at their own coach works, though some may have been built by Dodson. The six Straker-Squires were withdrawn in April 1907, but two returned to service in 1908. Several Milnes-Daimlers were converted for use as Royal Mail vans during 1907/8. The Dennis on trial was withdrawn in March 1906, but all the remaining buses were withdrawn during 1912 when they were replaced by TTA1s. In the list above, fleet numbers 3, 5, 7, 9, 10, 16, 17, 18, 19, 27 and 28 are probably correct for the vehicles described but are unconfirmed.

2 Tilling-Stevens Petrol-Electric TTA1 Type (1911-1923)

140 LN 9998	185 LE 9739	243 LF 9068	323 LF 9447	353 LF 9896	383 LH 8605*
141 LN 9775	189 LC 3787	244 LF 9414	324 LF 9448	354 LF 9897	384 LH 8606*
142 LE 9540	200 LC 4139	245 LF 9415	325 LF 9829	355 LF 9898	385 LH 8612*
143 LE 9547	201 LC 4144	246 LF 9416	326 LF 9830	356 LF 9899	386 LH 8613*
144 LE 9551	202 LC 4147	247 LF 9417	327 LF 9831	357 LF 9900	387 LH 8614*
145 LE 9556	203 LC 4148	248 LF 9418	328 LF 9832	358 LF 9901	388 LH 8615*
146 LE 9564	204 LC 4152	249 LF 9419	329 LF 9833	359 LF 9902	389 LH 8616*
160 LE 9652	205 LF 9012	300 LF 9420	330 LF 9834	360 LF 9903	390 LH 8617*
161 LE 9653	206 LF 9013	301 LF 9431	331 LF 9835	361 LF 9916	391 LH 8618*
162 LE 9654	207 LF 9014	302 LF 9432	332 LF 9837	362 LF 9917	392 LH 8619
163 LE 9655	208 LF 9015	303 LF 9433	333 LF 9836	363 LF 9918	393 LH 8620
164 LE 9656	209 LF 9016	304 LF 9434	334 LF 9838	364 LF 9919	394 LH 8621
165 LE 9657	210 LF 9017	305 LF 9435	335 LF 9839	365 LF 9920	395 LH 8622*
166 LE 9707	211 LF 9022	306 LF 9436	336 LF 9840	366 LF 9921	396 LH 8623
167 LE 9708	212 LF 9023	307 LF 9437	337 LF 9841	367 LF 9933	397 LH 8624
168 LE 9709	213 LF 9024	308 LF 9438	338 LF 9842	368 LF 9934	398 LH 8649
169 LE 9710	214 LF 9025	309 LF 9439	339 LF 9843	369 LF 9935	399 LH 8626
170 LE 9711	215 LF 9026	310 LF 9440	340 LF 9844	370 LF 9936	400 LH 8627
171 LE 9712	216 LF 9027	311 LF 9441	341 LF 9845	371 LF 9937	401 LH 8670*
172 LE 9717	217 LF 9028	312 LF 9442	342 LF 9846	372 LF 9938	402 LH 8671
173 LE 9718	218 LF 9043	313 LF 9821	343 LF 9847	373 LF 9958*	403 LH 8672*
174 LE 9719	219 LF 9044	314 LF 9822	344 LF 9848	374 LF 9959*	404 LH 8673
175 LE 9720	220 LF 9045	315 LF 9823	345 LF 9849	375 LF 9960*	405 LH 8674*
176 LE 9721	222 LF 9046	316 LF 9824	346 LF 9850	376 LF 9961*	406 LH 8675
177 LE 9722	223 LF 9047	317 LF 9825	347 LF 9851	377 LF 9962*	
179 LE 9734	237 LF 9048	318 LF 9826	348 LF 9852	378 LF 9963	
180 LE 9735	239 LF 9064	319 LF 9444	349 LF 9892	379 LH 8601*	
181 LE 9736	240 LF 9065	320 LF 9443	350 LF 9893	380 LH 8602*	
182 LE 9737	241 LF 9066	321 LF 9445	351 LF 9894	381 LH 8603*	
183 LE 9738	242 LF 9067	322 LF 9446	352 LF 9895	382 LH 8604*	

The first TTA1 entered service on 11th June 1911, and by May 1912, thirty-five of these buses had replaced all the older vehicles on route 12 and the two Lewisham routes. Another 81 were licensed between June 1912 and May 1913 for the new services operated from Victory Place and Lewisham. The last 58, which entered service from Acorn Street garage, were new between June and November 1913. All had 34-seat open-top bodies constructed by Tilling, and were instantly recognisable by the Renault style front bonnet. Five were mounted on secondhand TTA2 chassis in 1919/20. Those known are 310, 339 and 396.

Two buses (believed to be 347/8) were on loan to the Great Eastern Railway between April and November 1914 for a service between Harwich and Dovercourt. Five buses (347/8/53-5) were operated by Tilling in Brighton in 1915 but were returned upon the delivery of new buses. Another 22 (marked * in the list) were sent to Brighton in November 1916, but they gradually returned between 1920 and 1922, although 335 and 349 were also at Brighton for a time. All TTA1s were withdrawn from London service during 1921 and 1922 being replaced by TS3As.

Three garage lorries were built in 1914 and mounted on TTA2 chassis. They were Nos. 416 (LH 8659), 418 (LH 8660) and 419 (LH 8680). No doubt they were allocated to the three garages, Victory Place, Acorn Street and Lewisham, but 416 was later at Croydon, 418 at Catford and 419 at Brighton. A later lorry was 427 (LH 8724) on a TTB1 chassis.

3 Tilling-Stevens Petrol-Electric TS3A Type (1921-1931)
805 (XB 9960), 813 (XD 9131), 815 (XF 9270), 816-65 (XF 9801-50), 866-99 (XH 9251-84), 916-31 (XH 9285-300), 932-81 (XL 1201-50), 982-94 (XM 1401-13).
These 166 buses were of normal control and carried 48-seat open-top bodies with 22 passengers inside on forward-facing seats, and 26 on the top deck. The bodies were all built by Tilling. The first TS3A entered service on 9th July 1921 and 39 were in service by New Year's Day 1922. The last one was passed by the Metropolitan Police on 19th December 1922.

They were withdrawn between November 1930 and August 1931, being replaced by AEC Regents. No. 939 became a garage lorry at Croydon and 951 at Catford. Many of the others were purchased by showmen.

4 Tilling-Stevens Petrol-Electric TS7 O Type (1923-1933)
O 1-50 (XN 7301-50), O 51-100 (XP 2351-400), O 101-50 (XR 701-50), O 151-66 (XT 8773-88).
O 167 (XU 7070 – Bromley garage lorry)
These 166 forward control buses were purchased by LGOC and were numbered in a separate series from other Tilling buses. All had 48-seat bodies similar to those of the TS3As and constructed by Tilling, 121 at the Lewisham coach works, and 47 at Old Road, Lee including two spare bodies. The first TS7 entered service on 25th July 1923, and the last on 11th November 1924.

Eighty TS7s were withdrawn and either sold or scrapped between November 1932 and August 1933 following the introduction of the STL class. Forty-one TS7s were taken out of service during 1933, five being replaced by Regents taken from the Brighton fleet, but the others due to a reduction in service requirements consequent upon faster timetabling than the newer

Regents allowed. They were in store unlicensed when the Company's vehicles were taken over by LPTB in October 1933. At that time, there were 45 O type in service, being O 21-42/5/8/50/1/4/7/60/3/6/9/70/2/81/96, 150/5/9/61-6. In 1932/3, 25 Os were fitted with pneumatic tyres, being O 32/4/5/7/9-42/5/8/50/1/4/7/60/3/6/9/70/2/81/96, 150/5/9. Fifteen were at Croydon and 30 at Catford, but all were quickly withdrawn by the LPTB. Several were sold to showmen and nine were converted to tower wagons by the Board.

5 LGOC B Type single deckers operated by Tilling (1924-1925)
B 62 (LN 4762), B 489 (LN 288), B 1614 (LF 8394), B 4925 (LH 8482), B 4953 (LH 8464), B 4966 (LH 8555), B 4975 (LH 8469), B 4986 (LH 8487), B 4989 (LH 8476), B 4998 (LH 8473), B 5047 (LH 8556), B 5062 (LH 8497), B 5067 (LH 8503), B 5112 (LH 8544), B 5120 (LH 8496).
These LGOC buses had originally been double deckers but had been fitted with new 26-seat single-deck bodies in 1921/2. Ten of them had been allocated to route 109 from Nunhead (AH) for some time but were transferred to Bromley on loan on 7th May 1924. During 1925, B 4966 and B 5047 had replaced B 489, B 1614 and B 4953 which were transferred elsewhere, and the last 12 B types were withdrawn in October 1925 when single-deck O types were delivered.

Six similar B types had been loaned to Tilling at Croydon garage for route 71 between April and October 1922. Four of these are believed to be B 4933 (LH 8391), B 5036 (LH 8559), B 5126 (LH 8582) and B 5127 (LH 8567).

6 Tilling-Stevens Petrol-Electric Single-Deck TS7 O Type (1925-1932)
O 168-79 (XW 9888-99).
These 12 single deckers had been purchased by the LGOC to replace the B types on route 109. They carried Tilling-built 30-seat bodies and entered service in October 1925. At first, they were painted in LGOC livery with the GENERAL fleetname, but in March 1930 they were licensed by Tilling and repainted with their fleetname and livery. Between May and September 1929, they were fitted with pneumatic tyres. Withdrawal was in October and November 1932 when replaced by new AEC Regal T types.

7 Timpson Omnibus Services Ltd (1926-1928)
Eighteen Straker-Squire and two Frost Smith petrol-electric buses were acquired from Alexander Timpson & Sons on 25th March 1926, and Tilling operated these from Bromley garage.
The Straker-Squires were:—
31 (XN 2556), 32 (XN 2558), 33 (XN 2263), 34 (XN 2557), 35 (XN 2555), 36 (XN 2554), 37 (XO 3947), 38 (XO 3948), 39 (XO 3946), 40 (XO 3949), 41 (XO 3951), 42 (XO 3950), 43 (XP 9696), 44 (XP 9697), 45 (XR 3516), 46 (XR 5747), 47 (XR 3517), 48 (XR 9417).
The Frost Smiths were:—
49 (XM 2057), 50 (XM 5761).
In July 1926, the bodies of 49 and 50 were transferred to two Straker Squire chassis which had been charabancs, namely 29 (XK 6806), 30 (MC 9827).

Numbers 34, 37, 38, 40 and 41 were passed to LGOC in 1927 in exchange for five Tilling-Stevens TS3 type buses taken over from Cambrian Landray Ltd, and these became 51-5 in the Timpson fleet. A Cambrian Landray charabanc was fitted with a bus body from number 29 in February 1926, becoming 56. Between March and September 1927, the bodies from the remaining 14 Straker-Squires were put on to Tilling-Stevens chassis which had previously been vans or charabancs in Tilling's fleet. These were numbered 59 to 72. After Timpson Omnibus Services Ltd was wound up on 1st January 1928, the 20 Tilling-Stevens buses were licensed by Tilling and repainted from the silver livery of Timpson into Tilling's own livery. They were renumbered in the Tilling fleet as follows:—

51 (IT 292) – 1213	60 (XH 8144) – 1220	67 (YK 2738) – 1227
52 (IT 293) – 1214	61 (XC 9437) – 1221	68 (YK 2736) – 1228
53 (IT 301) – 1215	62 (XH 9758) – 1222	69 (YK 2735) – 1229
54 (IT 302) – 1216	63 (XH 9759) – 1223	70 (XW 5321) – 1230
55 (XM 2992) – 1217	64 (YK 2739) – 1224	71 (XX 5260) – 1231
56 (XB 9888) – 1218	65 (YK 2737) – 1225	72 (XX 2329) – 1232
59 (XE 7856) – 1219	66 (YK 2734) – 1226	

All 20 were withdrawn in 1930 upon delivery of the AEC Regents.

8 Experimental Buses (1929)
Following the decision to replace the open-top buses with covered-top vehicles, Tilling experimented with various types of covered-top bodies on loaned chassis, both in London and Brighton. Of these experiments, three were operated in London, they were:
3000 GU 7750 Tilling-Stevens TS17A (52-seat covered-top body by Tilling)
3001 GU 6483 Tilling-Stevens TS17A (52-seat covered-top body by Tilling)
      UU 9161 AEC Regent (51-seat covered-top body by Shorts)
   All three were in service on route 36, GU 7750 from 18th May 1929, UU 9161 from 28th July 1929, and GU 6483 from 11th October 1929. The AEC Regent saw service for a time in Brighton. The TS17A chassis were returned to the makers, as Thomas Tilling decided to abandon the petrol-electric system and order Regents.
9 AEC Regent Fleet (1930-1933)
6013-6100   GJ 2013-2100   LPTB ST 837-924
6101-6136   GK 1001-1036   LPTB ST 925-960
6137-6198   GK 6237-6298   LPTB ST 961-1022
   In April 1933, five Regents were transferred from Brighton, being:
6225   GN 6225   LPTB ST 1023
6227   GN 6227   LPTB ST 1024
6228   GN 6228   LPTB ST 1025
6230   GN 6230   LPTB ST 1026
6236   GN 6236   LPTB ST 1027
   During 1930/1 Thomas Tilling bought 250 AEC Regent chassis with petrol engines for use in London (186 buses) and in Brighton (64 buses). Tilling built 52-seat bodies at their coach factories at Lewisham, Camberwell and Brighton, though some were built by Dodson to Tilling's design. The bodies provided seats for 25 passengers on the lower deck and 27 on the covered upper deck reached by an open staircase. The 186 London buses replaced the 166 TS3As and the 20 ex-Timpson TS3s. They were numbered in a new series starting at 6001 and the first 12 went to Brighton. The first London bus, 6013, entered service on route 36 on 27th June 1930 and the last one, 6198, was licensed on 1st July 1931.
   All were taken over by London Transport on 1st October 1933 and included in the ST class, being numbered from ST 837 as shown above. Four more

Regents, acquired from independent operators, were added to these by the LPTB and allocated to Croydon garage: ST 1028 (GJ 8501) ex-Chariot, ST 1029 (VX 7487) ex-Empire, ST 1030 (VX 7553) ex-Pro Bono Publico, and ST 1031 (GJ 3020) ex-Pembroke.
10 AEC Regal Single-Deck Fleet (1932-1933)
T 307 (GY 8419), T 308-18 (GY 8408-18).
These 12 AEC Regals were operated by Tilling on behalf of LGOC, replacing the single-deck TS7 O type for route 109. They were all numbered in the T-class from the start. They had Tilling-built forward-entrance 28-seat bodies and entered service between August and October 1932. They passed to London Transport on 1st October 1933. During March and April 1936 they were replaced at Bromley garage by the larger six-wheeled single-deck LTs and the 12 T type were transferred to Kingston (K) garage. The spare Tilling body after overhaul in September 1936 was mounted on T 370 (JH 5101) a bus acquired from St Albans & District. This was dismantled in October 1939 but the 12 T type were retained in service, being withdrawn between December 1948 and October 1949.

LPTB No.	Date New	Initial Allocation	Date Withdrawn	Final Allocation
T 307	8/31	TB	8/49	K
308	8/32	TB	10/49	
309	8/32	TB	12/48	A
310	9/32	TB	6/49	K
311	9/32	TB	2/49	AV
312	9/32	TB	8/49	K
313	10/32	TB	3/49	
314	10/32	TB	8/49	K
315	10/32	TB	1/49	T
316	10/32	TB	8/49	K
317	10/32	TB	5/49	AR
318	10/32	TB	12/48	SP

T 370 carried the spare Tilling body after overhaul in September 1936, and this was painted green. The vehicle saw service from Dartford, Hertford and Hemel Hempstead and was withdrawn at HH in 1939.

11 AEC Regent STL Type (1932-1933)
STL 51-80 (YY 5351-80), STL 81-110 (JJ 6281-6310), STL 111-130 (AGF 821-40).
In 1932 the LGOC decided to replace the remainder of the TS7 petrol-electric buses still owned by them, totalling 102, with new AEC Regent long wheelbase petrol-engined buses. For these Tilling built 56-seat bodies to an improved pattern with enclosed staircases. They were built in their own coachworks and were allocated LGOC fleet numbers STL 51-152. Only eighty were built, 72 in London and eight in Brighton, as the order for the last 22 was cancelled and numbers STL 131-52 were never used. The first one, STL 51, entered service 29th October 1932 and STL 130 in June 1933. All passed to London Transport on 1st October 1933, being used almost entirely from Bromley, Catford and Croydon garages.

Appendix B
Complete List of Routes Operated by Thomas Tilling Ltd

Column 1 lists the routes by number. Column 2 gives brief details of the termini. Column 3 indicates the date upon which Tilling's buses first operated the service. Column 4 shows the last date of Tilling operation (the letter C indicates that this was current at time of takeover). The Tilling operation may not however have been continuous and details are to be found in the main text. Column 5 shows whether the service was daily (D), weekdays (W), Sundays (S) or summer Sundays (SS). Column 6 shows the LGOC garages which shared operation, not necessarily continuously.

Early Routes

(1)	(2)	(3)	(4)	(5)	(6)
'Times'	Oxford Street – Peckham (High Street)	29.09.04	05.05.09	D	
	Lewisham – Peckham	14.01.06.	27.06.06	D	
	Catford – Peckham	28.06.06	27.07.07	D	
	Catford – Greenwich Pier	17.06.06	27.07.07	D	
21	Oxford Street – Sidcup ('Black Horse')	28.07.07	10.12.10	D	
13	Peckham – Harringay ('Queens Head')	06.05.09	15.09.09	D	P
	Oxford Street – Peckham (resumed)	16.09.09	19.03.10	D	
13	Oxford Street – Bromley (Market Place)	20.03.10	10.12.10	D	
	Oxford Street – Peckham (High Street)	12.12.10	07.05.11	W	
	Lewisham – Sidcup ('Black Horse')	12.12.10	22.05.12	W	
	Lewisham – Bromley (Market Place)	12.12.10	20.07.12	W	
	Oxford Street – Sidcup ('Black Horse')	18.12.10	see no.63	S	
	Oxford Street – Bromley (Market Place)	18.12.10	see no.64	S	

Later Routes

(1)	(2)	(3)	(4)	(5)	(6)
1	Willesden ('White Hart') – Lewisham (Lewis Grove)	12.12.23	11.07.24	D	
1	Willesden ('White Hart') – Lewisham (Rennell St)	12.07.24	14.04.25	D	
1	Wembley Exhibition – Lewisham (Rennell Street)	11.06.24	01.11.24	W	P,AC
1	Willesden – Sidcup ('Black Horse')	20.04.24	09.11.24	S	P
1	Willesden – Chislehurst ('Queens Head')	01.06.30	02.10.32	SS	
1	Willesden – Green Street Green	14.04.33	C	SS	
1B	Willesden – Sidcup ('Black Horse')	10.04.25	14.11.25	SS	
1B	Willesden – Chislehurst ('Queens Head')	20.06.26	29.09.26	SS	
1C	Willesden ('White Hart') – Lewisham (Rennell St)	15.04.25	C	D	
10	Elephant & Castle – Wanstead ('The George')	07.07.13	28.03.14	D	G
10A	Elephant & Castle – Buckhurst Hill	29.03.14	24.01.15	D	G
10B	Elephant & Castle – Wanstead via Forest Gate	02.11.14	29.11.14	D	
12	Turnham Green – Peckham (High Street)	08.05.11	04.10.11	W	V
12	Turnham Green – Peckham Rye ('Kings Arms')	05.10.11	06.07.13	W	V
12	Turnham Green – Nunhead ('Waverley Arms')	07.07.13	22.04.14.	W	V
12	Shepherds Bush – South Croydon ('Red Deer')	19.05.29	C	S	ED
12A	Shepherds Bush – Penge ('Crooked Billet')	18.01.22	21.03.22	D	AH
12A	Oxford Circus – South Croydon ('Red Deer')	22.03.22	C	W	AH, ED
12B	East Acton (Ducane Road) – Lwr Sydenham (Bell Gn)	16.04.24	30.11.24	D	AH, S to 112
12C	Oxford Circus – Dulwich ('The Plough')	03.11.24	10.05.32	W	
12E	Shepherds Bush – South Croydon ('Red Deer')	01.12.24	12.05.29	S	AH, Q, ED
19A	Highbury Barn – Thornton Heath	30.03.23	14.10.23	S	B
19A	Highbury Barn – South Croydon	21.10.23	13.04.24	S	B
20	Wood Green – Shooters Hill	10.04.25	14.10.28	SS	
20D	Wood Green – Old Kent Road	23.08.33	C	W	
21	Crouch End – Sidcup ('Black Horse')	07.12.14	07.07.15	D	AD
21	Wood Green ('Wellington') – Sidcup ('Black Horse')	08.07.15	19.03.17	D	AD
21	Wood Green ('Wellington') – Sidcup ('Black Horse')	05.09.23	30.11.24	D	AD to 21A
21	Wood Green – Farningham ('Bull')	02.04.26	14.10.28	SS	SP
21A	Crouch End – Shooters Hill	25.01.15	07.07.15	D	AD
21A	Wood Green – Shooters Hill	08.07.15	23.01.16	D	AD
21A	Wood Green – Shooters Hill	25.07.23	25.11.24	D	AD
21A	Wood Green – Sidcup ('Black Horse')	01.12.24	C	D	SP
21B	Wood Green – Farningham ('Bull')	29.08.23	15.04.24	D	
25	Victoria Station – Seven Kings	05.11.22	04.02.23	D	
34	Liverpool Street – South Croydon ('Swan & Sugar Loaf')	03.11.24	26.03.29	W	H
35A	Camberwell Green – Walthamstow (Wood Street)	13.11.13	30.07.16	D	T

36	West Kilburn – Catford (Town Hall)	20.06.12	10.01.14	W	K
36	West Kilburn – Hither Green Station	25.01.15	C	D	
36	Willesden (Pound Lane) – Hither Green Station	07.09.19	22.02.20	S	AC
36A	West Kilburn – Grove Park Station	13.08.17	24.03.21	D	AC
36A	Camden Town Station – Grove Park Station	08.06.21	25.10.21	D	Q
36A	Camden Town – Bromley	26.10.21	14.02.22	D	Q
36A	West Kilburn – Grove Park Station	21.03.22	30.11.24	D	Q, P to 136
36A	Wembley Exhibition – Grove Park Station	07.05.24	01.11.24	W	
37	Isleworth (Market Place) – Peckham (High Street)	02.11.14	22.01.16	D	P, AB
37	Isleworth (Market Place) – Peckham (High Street)	05.11.22	25.03.23	W	
39	Victoria Station – ('Black Horse')	23.05.12	16.07.13	W	P
39	West Kensington – Sidcup ('Black Horse')	17.07.13	15.10.13	W	P
39	West Kilburn – Sidcup ('Black Horse')	16.10.13	06.12.14	W	P
39	North Finchley – Grove Park Station	07.05.19	02.09.19	D	
39	Hendon ('Bell') – Farnborough ('George & Dragon')	03.09.19	10.12.19	D	
40	Elephant & Castle – Upton Park	02.11.14	29.11.14	D	G
40A	Elephant & Castle – Wanstead ('The George')	30.11.14	24.01.15	D	G
42	Camberwell Green – Finsbury Park	29.06.14	19.03.17	D	J
43	Muswell Hill – South Croydon ('Swan & Sugar Loaf')	23.10.21	04.12.21	S	AK
43	Colney Hatch Lane – South Croydon ('Swan & Sugar Loaf')	11.12.21	07.04.22	S	AK
43	Colney Hatch Lane – Caterham	14.04.22	28.10.22	S	AK
43A	Muswell Hill – Peckham Rye ('Kings Arms')	05.07.14	09.08.14	SS	J
43A	Highgate – Peckham Rye ('Kings Arms')	29.06.14	12.08.14	W	J
47	Shoreditch Church – Bromley (Market Place)	20.07.12	12.04.13	D	
47	Bromley – Farnborough ('George & Dragon')	09.03.13	12.04.13	D	
47	Shoreditch Church – Farnborough	13.04.13	30.11.24	D	D to 47A
47	Shoreditch Church – Green Street Green	16.04.24	C	D	D
47A	Shoreditch Church – Bromley Common ('Crown')	02.11.14	30.11.24	D	D to 47B
47A	Shoreditch Church – Farnborough	01.12.24	C	D	D, H
47B	Shoreditch Church – Bromley Common ('Crown')	01.12.24	C	D	D
49	Shepherds Bush – Streatham Common	09.11.24	30.11.24	S	V
49	Shepherds Bush – Crystal Palace	15.06.24	02.11.24	S	V
49	Shepherds Bush – Lewisham ('Duke of Cambridge')	07.12.24	05.04.25	S	AK from 49A
49A	Shepherds Bush – Lewisham ('Duke of Cambridge')	09.11.24	30.11.24	S	AK
49A	Shepherds Bush – Streatham Common	07.12.24	05.04.25	S	V from 49
49B	Shepherds Bush – Crystal Palace	10.04.25	01.11.25	S	
49C	Shepherds Bush – Lewisham (Rennell Street)	08.11.25	C	S	
53A	South Hampstead (Swiss Cottage) – Abbey Wood	09.11.24	30.11.24	S	to 153
54	Oxford Circus – South Croydon ('Swan & Sugar Loaf')	13.02.24	10.06.24	W	P
54	Lewisham – South Croydon ('Swan & Sugar Loaf')	17.02.24	13.04.24	S	
54	Elephant & Castle – Riddlesdown ('Rose & Crown')	20.04.24	08.06.24	S	
54A	Charing Cross – South Croydon ('Swan & Sugar Loaf')	11.10.22	18.12.22	D	
54A	Strand (Aldwych) – South Croydon ('Swan & Sugar Loaf')	27.12.22	27.03.23	W	
54A	Elephant & Castle – South Croydon ('Swan & Sugar Loaf')	23.12.23	23.03.23	S	
54A	West Kilburn – South Croydon ('Swan & Sugar Loaf')	28.03.23	12.02.24	W	AH
54A	Lewisham – Riddlesdown	30.03.23	13.04.24	S	
55	Shoreditch Church – South Croydon ('Swan & Sugar Loaf')	08.06.13	01.11.14	D	
58	Camden Town Station – Chipstead Valley Road	31.03.29	C	D	P
59	Oxford Circus – South Croydon ('Red Deer')	23.01.16	31.03.17	W	
59	Camden Town Station – South Croydon ('Red Deer')	29.01.16	01.04.17	S	
59	Camden Town Station – South Croydon ('Red Deer')	02.04.17	18.10.21	D	
59	Camden Town Station – Kenley ('Kenley Hotel')	07.05.19	02.12.19	W	AK
59	Camden Town Station – Thornton Heath Clock Tower	19.10.21	05.12.22	W	N
59	Camden Town Station – Reigate	06.12.22	03.08.32	W	
59A	Oxford Circus – Caterham	14.08.16	17.03.17	W	
59A	Camden Town Station – Caterham	16.04.16	13.08.16	S	
59A	Camden Town Station – Caterham	02.04.17	30.11.24	D	AK to 159
59A	Camden Town Station – Godstone ('Bell')	04.04.20	02.11.24	S	AK
59A	Camden Town Station – Coulsdon ('Red Lion')	01.12.24	C	D	AK
59B	Oxford Street – Reigate	14.08.16	17.03.17	W	
59B	Camden Town – Reigate	19.11.16	05.12.22	D	AK
59B	Camden Town – South Croydon	27.03.29	C	W	P
60	Herne Hill – Peckham Rye ('Kings Arms')	11.09.13	22.10.13	D	
60	Herne Hill – Wood Green (Perth Road)	23.10.13	28.03.14	D	AR
60	Herne Hill – South Tottenham (Cornwall Road)	29.03.14	28.06.14	D	AR
63	Oxford Street – Sidcup ('Black Horse')	18.12.10	04.01.14	S	
63	Oxford Circus – Brockley ('Lord Breakspear')	23.04.14	08.07.14	D	

63	Oxford Circus – Catford (Town Hall)	09.07.14	01.11.14	D	
64	Oxford Street – Bromley (Market Place)	18.12.10	12.10.13	S	
66	Bostall Woods – Bromley Common	16.01.24	15.04.24	D	
66	Plumstead Common – Bromley Common	16.04.24	10.06.24	W	
66	Bostall Woods – Green Street Green	20.04.24	08.06.24	S	
71	Lewisham – South Croydon ('Swan & Sugar Loaf')	12.04.22	10.10.22	D	
72	Woolwich (Free Ferry) – South Croydon ('Red Deer')	19.03.17	20.05.19	D	
72	Shoreditch Church – South Croydon ('Red Deer')	21.05.19	22.03.21	D	ex 75A
72	Charing Cross – South Croydon ('Red Deer')	23.03.21	17.01.22	D	
75	Woolwich (Free Ferry) – S Croydon ('Swan & Sugar Loaf')	15.12.12	22.01.16	D	
75	Woolwich (Free Ferry) – South Croydon ('Red Deer')	23.01.16	14.04.27	D	to 75F
75	Plumstead – South Croydon ('Red Deer')	29.05.16	21.10.19	D	
75	Abbey Wood – South Croydon ('Red Deer')	16.02.21	30.03.22	D	
75	Woolwich (Free Ferry) – Coulsdon ('Red Lion')	15.04.27	12.10.27	S	
75	Woolwich (Free Ferry) – Godstone ('Bell')	31.03.29	02.10.32	S	
75A	Woolwich – South Croydon ('Red Deer') via Forest Hill	23.01.16	18.03.17	D	to 72
75A	Plumstead Station – Lower Sydenham (Bell Green)	18.03.18	30.11.18	D	
75D	Woolwich (Free Ferry) – Caterham Valley	27.03.29	C	D	
75F	Woolwich (Free Ferry) – South Croydon ('Red Deer')	16.04.27	26.03.29	D	
78	Shoreditch Church – Dulwich ('Grove Hotel')	02.03.13	02.09.19	D	P
78	Shoreditch Church – Dulwich ('Grove Hotel')	11.06.24	30.11.24	D	Q to 78A
78	Shoreditch Church – Bromley Common ('Crown')	10.04.25	15.11.25	S	
78	Shoreditch Church – West Wickham ('Wheatsheaf')	04.11.31	C	D	AH
78A	Shoreditch Church – Bromley Common ('Crown')	15.06.24	02.11.24	S	
78A	Shoreditch Church – Dulwich ('Grove Hotel')	01.12.24	C	D	Q, AH
91	Lewisham – Shooters Hill (Well Hall Road)	07.08.16	17.09.16	D	
91	Plumstead ('Plume of Feathers') – Brockley	18.09.16	18.03.17	D	
91	Plumstead – Sydenham Station	19.03.17	12.08.17	D	
92	Lewisham – Shooters Hill	07.07.13	06.12.14	D	
93	Sidcup ('Black Horse') – Woolwich ('Earl of Chatham')	19.03.17	20.10.17	D	
98	Peckham (High Street) – Honor Oak	19.03.17	25.05.17	D	
109	Penge (Tram Terminus) – Chislehurst ('Queens Head')	07.05.24	17.02.25	D	
109	Penge ('Crooked Billet') – Eltham (South End Lane)	16.06.26	30.05.33	D	SP
109	Penge – Welling ('Guy Earl of Warwick')	31.05.33	C	D	ED
109A	Penge ('Crooked Billet') – Chislehurst ('Queens Head')	18.02.25	15.06.26	D	
109D	Penge – Chislehurst ('Queens Head')	03.09.30	30.05.33	D	
112	East Acton – Lower Sydenham (Bell Green)	01.12.24	04.06.29	D	AH, S
112	Park Royal – Lower Sydenham (Bell Green)	09.06.29	26.01.30	S	M
112	Harlesden ('Willesden Junction Hotel') – Lwr Sydenham	02.02.30	01.11.31	S	R
112	Harlesden ('Willesden Junction Hotel') – E. Dulwich	08.11.31	C	S	S
112A	Park Royal – East Dulwich ('Grove Hotel')	05.06.29	C	W	S, AH
112A	Harlesden ('Willesden Junction Hotel') – E. Dulwich	29.01.30	10.05.32	W	S, AH
112C	East Acton – East Dulwich ('Grove Hotel')	03.11.31	C	W	S, AH
112E	East Acton (Ducane Road) – Lower Sydenham (Bell Green)	05.06.29	02.11.31	W	S,AH,
120A	Sudbury Town Station – East Dulwich ('Plough')	18.02.25	07.04.25	W	
132	Lewisham (Rennell Street) – Dartford (Westgate Road)	20.06.26	10.10.26	S	SP
136	Lewisham – Keston – Westerham Hill ('Fox & Hounds')	16.04.24	30.11.24	D	to 146
136	West Kilburn – Grove Park Station	01.12.24	07.04.25	D	
136	West Kilburn – Bromley Common	15.05.29	C	D	
136A	West Kilburn – Grove Park Station	08.04.25	14.05.29	D	
146	Lewisham – Westerham Hill ('Fox & Hounds')	01.12.24	C	D	
146A	Lewisham – Keston ('The Fox')	01.12.24	C	D	
146B	Lewisham – Downe (High Street)	31.05.33	C	D	
147	Shoreditch Church – Knockholt Pound	23.05.26	C	D	
152	Stockwell ('Swan') – Caterham	23.05.20	03.10.20	S	
153	South Hampstead (Swiss Cottage) – Abbey Wood	07.12.24	13.06.26	S	
159	Camden Town Station – Godstone	01.12.24	28.03.29	D	
159A	Camden Town Station – Caterham	01.12.24	28.03.29	D	
159C	Oxford Circus – South Croydon	20.05.31	C	D	
175	Plumstead Common – South Croydon ('Red Deer')	02.04.26	16.05.26	S	
213	Plumstead Common – Westerham Hill	23.05.26	04.10.31	S	
236	South Hampstead – Farnborough ('George & Dragon')	31.03.29	29.09.29	S	AH
254	South Croydon ('Swan & Sugar Loaf') – Croham Heights	16.12.31	14.03.33	D	
254	South Croydon ('Swan & Sugar Loaf') – Selsdon	15.03.33	C	D	
289	Plumstead Common – Green Street Green	13.04.30	05.10.30	S	
289A	Plumstead Common – Bromley Common	25.03.26	C	D	

Appendix C
Notes on Thomas Tilling's Motor Bus Tickets

When Tilling first started using motor buses on its Peckham/Oxford Circus route, which was in conjunction with the Atlas & Waterloo Association, the company continued the system of tickets that was in use on its horse bus services, using a similar layout of typeface. Being a joint operation, the tickets did not carry Tilling's own title, but used 'OMNIBUS TICKET' instead. They even continued the distinctive arrow to indicate UP or DOWN direction of travel (even if the arrows did face upwards for the down journeys and downwards for the up!) However, after the breakaway from the association, Tilling used its own title for the newly commenced motor services, including the long route from Oxford Circus to Sidcup. Tickets for this route departed from the 'menu' type of layout used previously, in that two lines of stages were used, one down each edge of the ticket, journeys 'up' to Oxford Circus on the left and 'down' to Sidcup on the right. Each stage was fully geographical, giving both the boarding point and the limit of availability in the one box. There were occasions when, for one reason or another, additional duties had to be worked or the normal tickets were not available and special tickets were brought into use. These did not bear any stage names, purely numbers (1-27) on each edge. A full range of values was produced for these numerical tickets, rising in halfpenny steps from ½d to 9d. Similar tickets were produced for the shorter routes, these carrying the numbers 1 to 10 only on each side.

After the agreement had been made with the LGOC in 1912, Tilling ceased to produce its own tickets, using those printed for, and supplied by, the LGOC for each particular route. These tickets were almost identical with those in use by the larger company in that they were of the fareboard type of layout, whereby only one stage name appeared in each box, that of the stage boarded, with the point of availability being directly opposite. The only difference was that once again the title 'OMNIBUS TICKET' was used. This form of ticket remained in use, with only minor variations, until around 1924 when, for routes operated solely by, or jointly with, Tilling, the title was changed to 'L.G.O.Co.Ltd. & ASSOCIATED Cos.' preceded by the word 'THE' in the case of tickets longer than the standard 2¼in or 2½in. On the smaller tickets the title was in a serifed upper case typeface — on the larger, non-serif. Around 1927/28, when the LGOC was absorbing many of the independent operators who had come onto the London streets in the early 1920s, it was decided that tickets for all routes, whether solely LGOC or not, should bear the associated companies title. With this standardisation, the word 'THE' was dropped from the longer tickets, and on the shorter varieties a bolder, non-serif type was adopted, which continued without alteration until the advent of the London Passenger Transport Board in July 1933.

Tickets are shown in order of mention in the text.

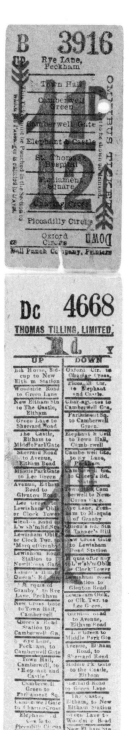

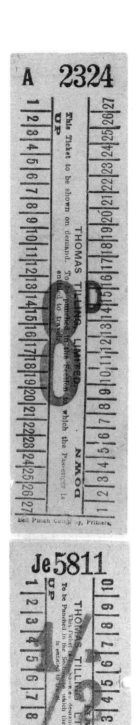